Are there Fundamental principles in Geographic Information Science?

Tobler Lecture Event 2012

With contributions from
Nicholas Chrisman, Andrew Frank & Dan Sui

Preface by
Waldo Tobler

Afterword by
Michael Goodchild

Edited and Introduced by
Francis Harvey

If we knew what it was we were doing, it would not be
called research, would it?
Albert Einstein

Are there fundamental principles in geographic information science?
Published 2012
Editor: Francis Harvey
Contributeors: Waldo Tobler, Andrew Frank, Nicholas Chrisman, Dan Sui, Michael Goodchild

ISBN: 1478213620
ISBN-13: 978-1478213628

This book is also available at Amazon.com in ebook format for Kindle readers on both Kindle devices and device independent software).

More information about formats and purchasing options are described at: http:// gisci-concepts.org

Table of Contents

Preface

Waldo Tobler
University of California at Santa Barbara
tobler@geog.ucsb.edu

The Association of American Geographers has numerous special interest groups. Many of these compete for space at the annual meeting by selecting speakers for one or more dedicated sessions devoted to their subject. The Geographic Information Science and Systems Specialty Group has adhered to this tradition since 2008 by inviting an outstanding scholar to give a presentation at the annual meeting. They have honored me by referring to this as the "Tobler Distinguished Lecture in GIScience". The first three lectures in this series, I am happy to say, were presented by innovative original thinkers in the field of geography. Mark Armstrong from Iowa was the first, followed by David Mark from Buffalo, and then Andre Skupin from San Diego. In 2012, Francis Harvey organized the lecture in a somewhat different manner. He invited two prominent geographic information scholars to tackle a difficult subject, to be followed by a discussant. The result is what we have in the following pages.

The subject chosen by Professor Harvey is a complex one. He posed the question "Are there fundamental principles in GIScience?" I suppose that this question can be, or is, asked in every specialty, and indeed in every academic field. How disparate would the answers from Archaeology, Anthropology, Botany, Biology, Computer Science, etc., be? I imagine that there would be a great deal of overlap. The question has been asked before. The National Center for Geographic Information and Analysis, established by the National Science Foundation in 1988, reported on ten years of study in a 1997 document titled "Fundamental Research in Geographic

Information and Analysis". This document includes summaries of twenty-four technical reports covering too large a variety of subjects for me to detail here. The report on the "GIS Technology and Body of Knowledge" also addresses many of these questions.

So, what is fundamental? The included essays give some hints about this. I would like here to suggest only two fundamental geographic concepts. The first is that of geographic "scale", about which many books exist. All geographic phenomena, observations, and events are resolution dependent. This is well documented, and applies to both coastlines and human affairs. But, it also applies to events in time. Curiously, the term "scale" is not often applied to temporal data. Why not? Both are best referred to as problems of resolution, and studied from the point of view of spectral analysis and the sampling theorem. Certainly, the temporal resolution is as important as the spatial one, and perhaps even more complicated. The second fundamental concept can be summarized in the word "global". Local "place" is important, but so is the rest of the world. We cannot avoid this.

Turning now to the chapters in this book, I count a total of 196 references (with some duplicates), ranging from 1810 to 2012, heavily biased towards the latter date. This should adequately introduce the student to the literature, though much of it is perhaps difficult to obtain. This literature is a moving target, since the field is still evolving. I will not discuss the individual papers in detail, but I do have a few general comments. In particular, you cannot expect discrete lists of fundamental principles here, but rather a discussion of what shape they might take.

Andrew Frank, while at the University of Maine, was an early participant in the National Center for Geographic Information and Analysis, and he has contributed substantially to the field. His arguments and approach have not changed appreciatively during this long period, even as he introduced novel and fundamental details. Coming from an engineering background, he stresses the importance of dynamics to geography, and goes into some detail in this. Process, topology, and ontology list amongst his themes. I endorse the use of mathematical methods and use them myself, but must admit that my mathematical competence does not extend to material from the twentieth century. Here I note that mathematics, as a human endeavor, is constantly changing and is itself not a timeless thing. If his topic were attempted a hundred years from now, it would likely be approached very differently. Thus, Andrew's topics do not include such specific forefront things as fractals, chaos theory, cellular automata, Turing morphogenesis, agent-based structures, etc. Not all of these are passing fads.

I have known Nicholas Chrisman since the days of the Harvard computer mapping conferences of the 1960s. During these conferences he, almost invariably and while still a student, raised questions for discussion. His lively nature does not seem to have changed. I take it that "deflationary approach" in the title of his chapter means to "let the air out of the balloon", or to "burst the bubble". Does this imply that GIScience (GIS) is a bit like the tulip mania of 1637? Or, does that only refer to the subject of "fundamentals"? The next discussion seems to hinge on whether GIS should aim at understanding society or at changing it. Perhaps both?

An aside in Nick's chapter deals with the timeliness of geographic information. Recently, I have been studying Ravenstein's paper on the "Laws of Migration" from the Statistical Society Journal of 1885. In doing this, I cannot help but wonder whether anyone would look at my contributions (sic) in 127 years. The question then arises whether fundamental principles of GIScience are timeless. Chrisman then asks whether, as "fundamental principles", they are irrefutable. I do not see these arguments going anywhere useful, but Chrisman pursues them to a conclusion. As to the long discussion regarding the "first law of geography", my attitude is that the importance of this law is that it calls attention to the exceptions, nothing more, but it was useful in the context in which I had used it. Regarding Chrisman's comment about forgetting, one only needs to look at current bibliographies and their extreme tendency to cite virtually nothing older than twenty years. Perhaps this is wise, in that our ideas, constructs, information, and intentions change. Nick also rightly complains about the overemphasis on Euclidean geometry for a round world. We can see that Chrisman's questions still invite discussion!

Daniel Sui was the designated formal discussant for the two papers. Dan has the advantage of living in the "big data" and "open science" era. Henceforth, all our puny previous work may look obsolete, but hopefully still germane. He discusses both Frank's and Chrisman's papers in detail, but continues with a long treatment based in part on their comments before elaborating on their themes, and in some sense extending them. He sees both consolidation and expanding directions occurring in the widening field. In this conciliatory effort, he sees much work and many references. The emphasis on the role of beauty in research is also recognized in his quotations from Russell and others.

Einstein is reputed to have remarked that theory comes from thoughtful insight and guessing. GIScience seems a bit more down to earth (literally) than this. The materials presented here can provide pointers and discussion for students and practitioners of GIScience. We have here writings on fundamentals, mathematics, deflation, and conciliation. We also have many citations, for all of which we thank Francis Harvey and the three authors. It will be exciting to see what happens to the future of the field.

Introduction

Francis Harvey
University of Minnesota
fharvey@umn.edu

Are there fundamental principles in geographic information science? As Waldo Tobler points out in the preface, this is a complex question. To address expectations right away, this book may fail to provide an answer to the question for all readers. Behind this deceptively straight-forward question is the intent to return and stimulate engagements with what many might call central issues in geographic information science (GIScience). The contributions, based on Tobler Lecture 2012 presentations and papers, highlight the importance of engaging and discussing fundamentals when working in geographic information science. Although the issues have changed from 1960s publications emphasizing automation or analysis, much continues to be written about GIS principles together with functionality, and rightfully so. Yet there is also room and a need to consider principles for and by themselves. This book both looks back and looks forward at principles that GIScience invokes and how to resolve the many fundamental challenges of abstracting and representing spatial observations, data, and information. Science and challenges will change, but principles should provide some stability. Answers to the question will depend of what are, and even if there are fundamental questions will evolve. On that note, when they look back, future readers may perhaps find this book offers some milestones to help trace the development of the field.

For certainly, the nature and place of fundamentals in any science are open to discussion. They also remain core issues in teaching and defining a field's activities and broader contributions. In this vein, this book aims to support engagements with the principles of GIScience in teaching and research. Interestingly, while the GIScience field involves many principles, it highlights relatively few fundamentals, notably Tobler's First Law of Geography (TFL). Outright engagements with fundamental concepts of geographic knowledge and geographic information appear rather infrequently (for example: Anselin 1989; Berry 1964; Board 1967; Goodchild, Cova, and Yuan 2007). However, many other publications beyond this short list engage fundamental issues. For example, the UCGIS research agenda points out numerous fundamentals within its broad research agenda scope (Usery and McMaster, 2004). A book that solely engages GIScience principles seems overdue. For one, GIScientists often seek conceptual foundation to better understand the science. Second, pointing out fundamental principles during teaching can help students advance their learning. Third, users and researchers often look for help with fundamental questions lurking in the use of GIS technologies. In particular, the challenge of representation seems especially pertinent--and is evident in all contributions. As Michael Goodchild recently wrote, if there is a single challenging issue in GIScience research, it involves finding "useful and efficient ways of capturing and representing the infinite complexity of the geographical domain in the limited space and binary alphabet of a digital computer" (Goodchild 2011, 2442). The questions and approaches to GIScience principles raised in this book are perhaps just the modern formulations of discussions that people have been involved in for centuries and even millennia.

As readers will find, this book's three contributions take on the title question from a range of approaches. They expand, ground, and re-engage discussions of GIScience principles and also open ways to think about how each GIScientist chooses to engage fundamental principles of the field. The contributors have taken the liberty of tackling the title question in creative ways and bring a range of approaches and philosophical foundations to bear. The range and scope of the issues and challenges in their contributions open up interesting and thought-provoking perspectives.

To provide some orientation for readers to the contributions, I offer some brief notes connected to two questions to help guide readers. First, what are the contributors' key points? Second, what underlying or philosophical issues do they engage? In the book's first chapter, Andrew Frank proposes a framework to move GIScience to consider processes grounded in formal mathematical approaches. This conceptual framework speaks to the importance of developing fundamental principles through robust mathematical formalizations while retaining a clear grounding to empirical observations. This chapter also points to the elusiveness of "truth", the limits of logic, and imperfections of knowledge: tiers of ontological description support the separation of processes and corresponding rules. The grounding of ontological tiers facilitates the use of formal logic. As Frank explains, this conceptual framework is the basis for a spatial time machine that accounts for time/space dynamics. Difficulties remain with the interactions between physical and social realities as GIScience moves beyond the concept of GIS as a database for all possible maps.

The chapter by Nick Chrisman speaks to these last points as well. Following a deflationary approach (related to anti-essentialism and anti-interpretativism philosophies), Chrisman offers a different framework for considering developing principles that matter in GIScience in terms of their utility and relevance. His approach opens up three ways to think about GIScience fundamentals: (1) as concepts to examine and evaluate for their influence on ongoing work, (2) as a critique of mathematics and formal approaches as the superior way of knowing and developing multiple ways of scientific discovery, and (3) as a way to ground concepts in the complexity of practice.

Dan Sui, who took on the important challenge of commenting on earlier versions of the first two chapters at the Tobler Lecture event in February 2012, engages the important questions of who benefits and to what ends. He points to important linkages to big data and open science and suggests that the way forward for GIScience involves broader engagements with both mathematical concepts and critical assessments. Following Sui, and building on their exchanges, the frameworks and approaches Frank and Chrisman provide readers offer a complementary way forward that accounts for different forces. Indeed, as Andrew Frank lays out in his persuasive chapter, while mathematics is the most widely used scientific means to represent the world, our observations remain imperfect, and mathematical truth remains limited. Nick Chrisman is less sanguine and is instead concerned that the complexities of the world and its representation require a deflationary approach, one that accepts principles, observations, or characteristics neither at face value nor as absolutes. The differences and complementary elements in these approaches suggest the value of engaging fundamental principles from a range of perspectives. The engagements with each other's work additional provide some openings for reflecting on broader discussions and developing the field further.

Still, without a single answer to the title question of this book, some readers may wonder, what then is its contribution? Teaching GIScience often involves an introduction to the key principles of the field that fix protagonists and opponents. Scientific discussions of fundamentals in many fields appear to revolve around paradigms (Kuhn, 1962) and disciplinary questions. This book has these discussions, especially in the classroom, in mind. Even with an emphasis on teaching GIS functions, fundamental principles remain the bread and butter of GIScience education, and most classrooms serve as greenhouses where fundamentals are connected to functions, breeding novel and innovative approaches. GIScience researchers have developed multiple ways to address fundamental challenges. Instead of just clashes between paradigms, following Galison's (1998) seminal study of the progress made in high energy physics during World War II, work in science usually lies in the creation of productive trading zones between different approaches (see Harvey 2005 for a discussion of this concept in connection to interoperability). As Dan Sui points out in his contribution, Big Data and Open Science research both offer current areas for these trading zones to develop.

Moving on to other issues for this introduction to cover, a few explanations and expressions of gratitude are in order. To begin, I would like to speak my strongest gratitude to the contributors for their time and willingness to prepare papers for this book. Beyond Andrew Frank, Nick Chrisman, and Dan Sui, I also want to thank Waldo Tobler and Michael Goodchild for their immediate willingness to prepare contributions that provide a framework for the book. I also want to thank Kate Beard, Werner Kuhn, Harvey Miller, Seth Spielman, Matt Duckham, Martin Raubal, Christian Kray, and

Angela Schwering for their help in conceiving, organizing, and preparing the Tobler Lecture event. The annual Tobler Lecture event is organized by the Association of American Geographers (AAG) Geographic Information Systems and Science Specialty Group (GISS-SG).

The production of this book has taken roughly one year from inception. The contributions from Frank, Chrisman, and Sui were presented first at the 2012 Tobler Lecture event. These three contributors were contacted in late summer 2011 and invited to participate in the Tobler Lecture and book. They shared draft versions of the chapter-length texts before the event to help facilitate their writing and discussions at the event. They originally presented draft versions at the AAG Conference in New York City on 26 February 2012. After the Tobler event, contributors revised their drafts in spring and early summer 2012. Copy-editing, additional editing and production were completed in August 2012.

I also want to make several points about the distribution and contents of this book. It appears as publishing in general is adapting to digital media. Stepping back from those changes, I want to point to the CATMOG series and a short publication series published by the AAG some 30 years ago as the models for smallish and very focused books aimed at a large numbers of readers and at a low cost. Utilizing current modes of distribution, this book is provided both in eBook and in print formats. The contents are the same, although obviously the pagination will vary (which is also why there is no index). The specific rationale for publishing this book as an eBook in addition to its print format is to reach as many GIScience students and researchers as possible at the lowest possible cost. By holding expenses low, organizing the production and imprint directly, particularly as an eBook, it is possible to further hold down the costs. This should benefit future Tobler Lectures: all proceeds from the sales of this book (after modest production expenses) go to the Association of American Geographers (AAG) Geographic Information Systems and Science Specialty Group to help support expenses arising in the organization of the annual Tobler Lecture at the annual AAG meeting and conference. Please consider helping to support the Tobler Lecture series by recommending additional purchases of this book.

At this point, I also want to add a brief note about intellectual property rights and this book. As many readers are certainly aware, academic publishing is undergoing many changes. The book, in both eBook and print formats, is published under the Creative Commons Attribution-NonCommercial 3.0 (CC BY-NC 3.0) arrangement. Under a Creative Commons (CC) License, the authors retain all rights to their work. The CC license specifies the conditions for the use of their work. Under this particular license, readers are allowed to copy, share, and adapt this book and its chapters for any non-commercial purpose as long as they attribute the editor and/or author appropriately. For other uses you need to contact the authors and me directly. If you are interested in learning more about CC licenses (and the other options), visit http://creativecommons.org. You can contact me directly with questions or comments about the production and book.

To help support continued engagements with the book's contributions, I also want to point readers to a web site with more information about the book and links to forums for discussions about the *Principles* book as well as related work: gisci-concepts.org.

Finally, I would like to conclude the introduction with a final note related to discussion of fundamental concepts that I found vivid in many exchanges with GIScience colleagues over the years. This point, which drove the organization of the Tobler lecture event 2012 and publication of this book, echoes the sentiment fromMichael Goodchild's afterword: while unlikely that a single list of fundamental concepts for GIScience ever emerges, we are sure to find more commonality in developing our own lists and discussing fundamentals. Asking questions about fundamental principles helps reveal and refine the principles that help guide research, provide foundations for future scholarship, and develop GIScience.

GIS Theory - the fundamental principles in GIScience: A mathematical approach

Andrew U. Frank
Technical University of Vienna
frank@geoinfo.tuwien.ac.at

1. Fundamentals must be valid for a long time

Waldo Tobler, in discussing what distinguishes fundamentals, aimed to identify principles that remain valid for at least twenty years, and I used a similar guideline in selecting topics for my GIS Theory class (Tobler 1976). The desire to find what is valid for an extended future can serve not only as a practical guideline of what should be taught, but also as an approach to research topics. Issues that are technology dependent may be important, but they are hardly fundamental.

The desire for long-lasting principles makes me turn to mathematics as a timeless science not influenced by the rapid development of technology. Mathematics serves as the foundation to nearly all sciences and is definitely relied on by GIScience (Golledge 2008). The question GIScience poses is how to extend the formal methods of mathematics to apply to geography. Geography is about space and processes in space (Abler et al. 1971). Change is what was important for humans, early on, to guard against swiftly moving predators, and now change is what grabs both the public's and the politicians' attention (Frank 1998). Mathematics has several theories about space; this essay will explore how these--not always compatible-- theories apply to geographic space. GIS are databases reporting about objects with spatial references (Frank 1988), but GIS must progress to the dynamic description of the world: states and processes changing the states. The GIS must produce "movies" of the changes in the past, not just the current state, and it must include methods to produce simulations of possible future developments under specified assumptions. This could be called a "spatial time machine" (Wells 1895). Partial solutions for specific applications have been studied (e.g., Goodchild et al. 2007; Reitsma and Albrecht 2005), but terminology, approaches, and formalization methods remain confused (Galton 2008). The dominance of static representations of the world in current GIS software packages makes, for example, integration with business software, which includes dynamic models of business processes (e.g., Service Oriented Architecture (SOA)), difficult (Treiblmayr et al. 2012).

The chapter starts with the premise that geography (as a science) is about spatial process and finds that GIS and GIScience today is too much influenced by the classic database paradigm of static representation of state (Ullman 1988). I assume that simple processes combine to create more complex processes and focus, therefore, on the methods to combine processes. Combination rules for processes are crucial for liberating GIS from the current static view to become spatial time machines (i.e., systems which analyze and present the evolution of spatial patterns in time, from the past to the future). To achieve this, three paradigm changes (Kuhn 1962; Kuhn 1970) are necessary:

1. Focus on the representation of a changing world in a GIS.
2. Accept the unavoidable and beneficial imperfection in our knowledge.
3. Construct models as combinations of simple processes and systematically explore the methods for combinations.

I turn to mathematics and analyze first the role formal mathematical approaches can play in GIScience and show, as an example, how functors construct more complex algebraic structures from simpler ones, like rational numbers from integers or focal operations on layers in map algebra from simple operations on values. Note that a mathematical structure (which is what is understood by structure throughout this chapter) is a set of things with operations applicable to them; their operations are described by the effects they have on the things. In the same vein, A review of geometry and topology shows how operations to construct complex figures are built from simple operations on points.

The combination approach is not limited to geometry: a tiered ontology, for example, describes concepts that can be combined, where each component is simpler to understand than the whole. The essay concludes with a refinement to the premise: geography (as a science) is about spatial processes and how they combine in space and time, indicating that the question--how processes interact--is equally important as the mere description of spatial processes.

2. The World is a Complex Thing: Complexity Emerges from the Arrangement

My complexity assumption is that the complexity I observe in the world is the result of the interaction between a very large number of small processes, but each process itself is simple. It is a philosophical question whether the processes are simple or conceived as simple, because humans can understand and construct models of simple base processes. The focus of the future GIS should not be on the static things, but on processes and how they interact. We use here, following a mathematical, algebraic tradition, the term (algebraic) "structure" for a set of related operations and the rules of their interaction; for example, the group structure includes an operation plus for integers, which follows the rules $a + b = b + a$, or $a + 0 = a$, etc. .

The research direction produced by the complexity assumption gives a focus on the (formal) description of generic methods for combination of processes, not the static combination of things. A complex process consists of an interacting combination of things and produces complex, observable behaviors from the simple behaviors of the constituent processes.

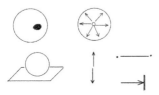

Figure 1: Image schemata for CONTAINER, CENTER-PERIPHERY, SUP- PORT, UP-DOWN, LINKAGE, and BLOCKAGE.

Image schemata represent cognitively salient processes. Lakoff and Johnson (Lakoff and Johnson 1980) have described a small number of basic processes, which are cognitively salient and used everywhere for metaphorically understanding observations. Some examples of importance for geography are shown in Figure 1 and discussed by Raubal (2001). The image schemata can be considered as examples for the simple processes from which the complex ones are constructed.

Image schemata dominate language: observe how prevalent the use of the image schema "up-down", with the meaning "up is good", is used in English: we give up, we pick up, etc. These image schemata are generalized to algebraic structures: containers are a refined form of sets, links give rise to graph theory, etc., as was shown by Lakoff and Nuñez (2000). The image schema has entailments, which follow from the salient static situation: from the statement "the apple is in the bowl" follows that there was a process that put it in, and another that can take it out of the bowl.

Take a car: It consists of a gas tank, an engine, and wheels. The gas tank is a container process, the engine a transformer of chemical energy in torque, etc. The car is a car because the processes interact, not because the static pieces are in some specific arrangement. The Marble Boat in the Beijing Summer Palace garden looks like a boat, and its components have the right form, but they are not functioning. Therefore, it is not a functional ship (see Figure 2)!

Figure 2: The Marble Boat (Source: http://commons.wikimedia.org/wiki/File:Barco_de_marmol_palacio_verano_pekin.jpg).

3. Methodological questions in GIScience: The Role of Mathematics and Formalization

Mathematics is a method for formalizing our understanding of the world. It has been applied successfully in the natural sciences to provide them with a methodical foundation; GIScience is one of the channels through which mathematical methods are brought to geography in order to further the quantitative approaches in geography.

3.1 What can Mathematics Contribute? - Formal Systems

A mathematical formal approach is routinely used in physical geography but can be used in social geography as well; it is understood that this is not necessarily quantitative, but mathematics also offers qualitative formalism. If we want to integrate our knowledge into a GIS, we cannot avoid being formal, because computer programs are necessarily formal and best described as machines manipulating symbols according to programmed rules. However, formal does not necessarily mean quantitative and does not imply deterministic!

In Chrisman's (2012) terminology, this is a Universalist position--but with a twist: it combines the limitations of mathematical universal truth in the symbolic realm and the recognition of the limitations of the grounding of symbols in reality. Perhaps this could be called a limited universalist stance.

Mathematics is a game played by processing symbols, and it cannot exist, per se, without grounding it in anything about the world. From statements assumed true and other statements follow, by logical deductions which can be checked; this makes mathematical truth (nearly) timeless, but this timeless truth is not related to the world.

3.2 Grounding Connects the Formal with the Real

Formal descriptions must be related to empirical observations of the world; this is often called "grounding" (Scheider 2009; Lakoff 1987). Only grounded statements have meaning with respect to reality. Grounding established the relation between the observable reality, the observations, and the formal system (see Figure 3). Grounding is necessary, firstly, when the observations are transformed into formal statements. Secondly, grounding is used when the conclusions from the formal deductions are translated into real-world terms. I call this closed loop semantics (see Figure 3).

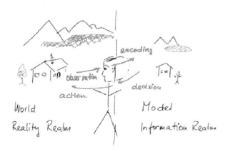

Figure 3: Closed loop semantics: the observation and encoding are checked by feedback from decisions and actions.

The physical and cognitive similarity between humans makes it possible for humans to agree on some basic terms (Wierzbicka 1996; Rizzolatti and Craighero 2004). This makes communication possible, but not perfect. Closed loop semantics are at work in all our interactions with the world, and thus help us to bring our personal conceptualizations in line with those of others. The feedback loop between the observation and encoding input path from the world to the GIS--and back through the decision and action output path from the GIS to the world--ensures that misinterpretations are identified and, over time, corrected.

3.3 Imperfection in our Knowledge

We must accept that observations of reality are imperfect, and that the translation of human, subjective observations to formal terms is fraught with problems. Therefore, the knowledge we have about reality is always imperfect.

I use the term "imperfection" as a superordinate to specific kinds of imperfections, like imprecise, inaccurate, error, etc. (Frank 2007). Imprecision is--contrary to frequently held beliefs--beneficial. With the reduction in information, which increases imperfection, humans can respond with short delays to the challenges the real world poses (Simon 1997). Without imperfection in the information we receive, we would be constantly suffering from information overload. For example, the imperfection in a regular 1:500'000 road map makes it useful for helping someone drive between major cities. It is terribly imperfect when compared with a detailed 1:25'000 map, but exactly this imperfection makes it suitable as a road map for driving, which the 1:25'000 map is not!

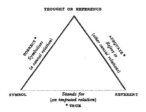

(a) The semantic triangle (after Ogden and Richards Ogden and Richards (1923), but goes back at least to Bolzano 1810)

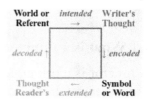

(b) In communication two triangles must be combined (afterSearle (1976)

Figure 4a and 4b: The semantic triangle and its combination to show process of communication. (Figure 4A from: http://en.wikipedia.org/wiki/File:Ogden_semiotic_triangle.png; Figure 4B from: http://en.wikipedia.org/wiki/Triangle_of_reference)

Problems exist regarding (1) limitations in the observations because measurements are always with some error, (2) classification, and (3) encoding. There is no direct connection between a formal term (or a natural language word) with the objects in the world--a dog is not more a "dog" than a "chien", "Hund", or any other name. The semantic triangle (see Figure 4; Ogden 1923; Eco 1976) shows that human perception and classification is always interfering between the object and the sign--the relation between object and sign is indirect and composed of several cognitive (subjective) processes (Frank 2008). The triangle shows only how one person connects symbols to referents; for communication, the speaker's process must be reversed in the listener (Searle 1976), as suggested in Figure 4b.

4. Example Combination with a Functor: Local Operations in Map Algebra

This section introduces a principled method often used in mathematics to combine known, simple things into more complex ones, such that it is a consistent extension. The GIS example used here for illustration is that Local Operations applied to layers in Map Algebra (Tomlin 1983) are the result of a functor taking simple operations between values (e.g. addition).

4.1 What is a Functor?

A functor is a principled method of extending a set of related processes, such that all operations and rules which held before the extension still applies after the extension, but more can be achieved with the extension than before (MacLane and Birkhoff 1991). Functors are widely used to extend operations to new domains, but seldom recognized as such. Everybody remembers how, in fourth grade, the problem of dividing three apples among four kids was solved through the introduction of rationals. Few realize much later that this is an example of the application of a functor to combine two integers to a rational.

Functors are used to create vector spaces, again as pairs of reals, but with different rules for the operations than for rationals. Compare the addition of rationals with the rule $a/b + c/d = (ad + cb)/bd$ with vector addition $(a,b) + (c,d) = (a+c, b+d)$. Functors can be used to construct vector spaces of any dimension. The point here is, again, that the functor is not only operating on the coordinates (the things), but also transforming operations (e.g., the operation convex hull from 2D to 3D; Karimipour 2008, 2009).

4.2 Local Operations are Produced by Functor

The local operations in Map Algebra (Tomlin 1983) are functions combining two values to produce a new value, which is applied to a layer. The domain of the function is originally a value (e.g., a real number) and should be applied to the new domain layer. In order to see this as a functor, the layers are conceived as functions from two indices x and y to a value: layer: $(x,y) \rightarrow v$.

Figure 5: A functor carries the operations combining elements to operations combining layers of a GIS (Navratil and Harnoncourt 2004).

The description of space, with properties as functions from a position in space and time, to a value is a fundamental concept in GIScience. A common example is a terrain model, where to each (x,y) pair belongs an h value (h = height $[x,y]$). A complete description of all properties in space can be made in this format: $v = \mathrm{f}(x,y,h,t)$ (Frank 1990; Goodchild 1992). The functor makes the operations on values applicable to the layers.

5. Abstract Space: Geometry and Topology

Geography is about process in space and time. Mathematicians use the concept of space very broadly. The question posed here is: what are the properties of the space in reality and how is it treated in a formal system? Mathematicians have addressed this question as "what is a geometry" (Blumenthal 1970), and have revealed fundamental properties of space, which differentiates space from time (Blumenthal 1986).

A useful definition is that geometry is a group of transformations (processes, operations), under which certain properties remain invariant. The algebraic structure group means that both a zero element (do nothing) and an inverse (transform back) exist. An example for such a group of transformations is rigid body motion, which describes the transformation when solid objects are moved; distances and angles between points remain the same, and ordinary Euclidean geometry results. Compare this with the movement of a flexible garment: movements leave only neighborhoods the same, but change distances and angles; this is an example where topology plays its role.

The approach I take here is one of showing how the different aspects of geometry used in GIS can be constructed from simpler processes to justify the "complexity assumption" mentioned before. The text here is a first sketch of such an approach; a stringent description could be a valid Ph.D. thesis topic!

5.1 Points in Space

A functor (see above) connects the domain of points and space-time points of arbitrary dimension from the continuous domain of real numbers. Additional vector operations are defined to identify right angles, distances, etc.

Often, spaces in mathematics are considered infinite and continuous, everywhere dense. This leads to nicer (simpler) theories, but causes two difficulties: it (1) contradicts experience--cutting paper in half cannot be done infinitely often--and (2) is impossible to implement on computers. Computers are finite machines with only a finite number of states (Asperti 1991).

The continuous space--as other continuous scales--must be mapped to finite domains. In GIS, two kinds of implementations, named "raster" and "vector", dominate the practice and lead to a large literature on an implementation problem blown up to a fundamental issue. Admittedly, the issue already confused the Greeks, as documented with the "Achilles and the Turtle" story (Hofstadter 1979).

The Harvard GIS group hit the problem of finite resolution early on when programming the intersection of two spatial subdivisions (Chrisman 1975). A modern solution, possible with the technology improvements, is to select rational numbers, formed with big integers; this gives an exact representation for geometry with straight line and does not exhibit problems due to internal approximations (Bulbul 2009a).

5.2 Infinite Objects Constructed Dimension Independent

Most studies of geometry are dimension specific; GIScience demands a dimension independent approach to bring together phenomena which are best described by concentrating on the dimensions important for them. Consider the different views of "coastal area": as a one-dimensional boundary between sea and land, as a two-dimensional beach area, as a three-dimensional water volume, etc. The world can be seen in different ways, but it is always the same world.

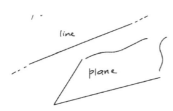

Figure 6: Infinite geometric objects of dimension one and two.

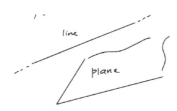

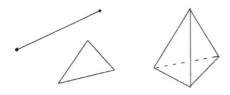

Figure 7: Finite geometric objects of dimension one, two, and three.

Tuples of points define infinite geometric objects: two points define a line (one-dimensional), three points generally position a plane (two-dimensional), etc. (see Figure 6). Blumenthal and Menger proposed an axiomatization of projective geometry with only two operations, namely 654892246 intersection and 654892246 *merge* with a few axioms (Blumenthal and Menger 1970); the emerging fundamental algebraic structure is now known as lattice (MacLane and Birkhoff 1991) and of great importance in GIS (Frank et al. 1997).

5.3 Finite Geometry

A "vector" GIS describes delimited spatial objects with coordinates. Tuples of points, with an interpretation different from the tuples which represent infinite objects, define the simplest finite geometric objects: one point is a 0-dimensional object, two points give a segment of a line, three points a triangle, four points a tetrahedron, etc. (see Figure 7)

This poses the question: What are the best geometric objects to represent geometry? I have advocated simplices, which combine to simplicial complexes, but cells and cell complexes are preferred because they produce less data. Additionally, simplices are not closed under intersection: the intersection of two simplices is not a simplex, but the intersection of two convex figures is convex. A novel suggestion is using convex figures, which combine in an alternate hierarchical decomposition (Bulbul and Frank 2009a).

5.4 Topological Spaces

"Topology matters, metric refines" (Egenhofer and Dube 2009): Topology is like doing geometry on a balloon: it abstracts from the details of metric information and preserves only the usually more important "overall Gestalt". Topology introduces the concept of neighborhood, which is preserved through topological (i.e. continuous) transformations--it is not permitted to cut, puncture, or glue. Boundaries separate regions--a term that is definable through neighborhood and being a neighbor--and are preserved through topological transformations. The topological relations between the geometry of geographic objects matter: Switzerland and Italy are neighbors; Great Britain is an island--the length of the border or the size of the island matters less than the relation.

(a) Political Map of Europe   (b) Neighborhood graph for European Union countries

Figure 8: The countries of Europe, reduced to a neighborhood graph (Figure 8a from: http://commons.wikimedia.org/wiki/ File:Europe_countries_map_en_2.png)

The map of the countries of Europe is reduced to their "important" relations, showing which countries are neighbors (Figure 8). This is a desirable reduction in information content: only the information important for the situation is preserved. Mathematicians use a construction of a forgetful functor to describe such mappings (MacLane and Birkhoff 1991).

Ordinary topology, or point set topology, treats space as an infinite collection of points; this is not suitable for representation and treatment in a finite computer. Therefore, one has to move to a higher level of abstraction, namely to algebraic topology, which focuses on counting discrete topological objects, typically simplices. Egenhofer has given an implementable definition of some important topological relations (Egenhofer and Franzosa 1991), which are essentially equivalent to the (non-constructive) RCC-calculus (Randell et al. 1992).

Simplicial complexes are just one method for combining simpler geometric objects to represent complex figures; the operations on the complex figure must translate to operations on the simpler geometric object from which the complex figure is composed. In a GIS, the intersection of two figures is probably the most important operation.

Bulbul and Frank have suggested an alternate decomposition with convex polytopes; convex polytopes are represented by lists of varying length of points, but the intersection of two convex polytopes is again a convex polytope. The number of convex polytopes a figure is composed of is--in general--much smaller than the number of simplices necessary for the same figure (Bulbul and Frank 2009c).

6. Populated and Used Space: The Physical and Social Realm

Ontology, in the sense of computer science, is about the (human) conceptualization of the reality; it includes mostly epistemological aspects (Guarino 1995). The focus is how to structure and represent knowledge. An ontology treats objects and processes on equal footing, assuming that the current static situation is the result of the processes active in the past. The focus is on asking questions about processes and the combination of processes to capture transformation of knowledge and imperfection from the observations to the decisions. The tiered ontology (Frank 2001) separates different levels of imperfection. The goal is to create descriptions that can be formalized, implemented, and used as guidelines for structuring application knowledge; relevant questions of mathematical formalism are discussed in the next section.

Are there fundamental principles in GIScience?

6.1 Tiered Ontology

Different processes help humans to acquire knowledge about the world. The processes can be organized as a sequence, where the results of lower-tier processes of acquisition of information are transformed--and typically reduced in detail--to higher tiers. The analysis of these information-reducing translations could use the formalization of a forgetful functor (MacLane and Birkhoff, 1991), which maps from one domain to another, preserving only information of interest.

Three major tiers of forms of being can be identified. Tier 1 is essentially the acquisition of raw, point-related data, with tier 2 the formation of physical objects with properties and tier 3 the social constructions, like money or marriage. These tiers coincide with different levels of imperfection in our knowledge and different approaches for the assessment of information quality (Frank 2008).

The tiers of the ontology describe different realms of knowledge, and different methods for their description apply. Different methods for the description and combination of process are preferred in each tier, and the kinds of imperfections in the different tiers require different treatment and safeguards to avoid invalid deduction.

There is no objective knowledge about reality--but some observations are less subjective than others, and some classifications are less influenced by subjectivity than others; the tiered ontology gives an explanation and an ordered classification that ranges from more objective to less objective. GIScience research has produced a large number of methods to deal with imperfections, especially statistical approaches to measurement errors, omissions, and commissions, fuzziness of classification, and context dependence of encoding. There is some confusion as to when to use which of the mathematically involved models. The tiered ontology indicates which of these models for imperfection applies when.

A tiered ontology results in a separation of processes and rules for composition in each tier and rules, which combine the tiers to a single ontology; the different tiers describe the same physical world--and there is only one! Objects and processes in one tier must map to processes in the other tiers. Two examples (see Table 1): (1) the social process of "paying for coffee" (tier 3) is the physical process of moving some pieces of metal from my pocket to the pocket of the waiter in the coffee shop (tier 2), which could be described as a Partial Differential Equation (PDE; tier 1); (2) a hailstorm described by a PDE in tier 1 that is a weather event in tier 2 and finally an "insured event" that leads to payment to a farmer in tier 3.

tier			example "buying coffee"	Example "Hail"
1	Point observation	object	Metal volume	Water volume
		process	Moving in force field	Falling in gravity
2	Physical objects	object	coin	Hail corn
		process	Transfer of coin from me to waiter	Hail corns falling
3	Social constructions		Payment for coffee	Insured hail event

6.2 Physical World

Raw observation of the physical world helps researchers collect values for properties at a certain location at a certain time (e.g., temperature $v = \mathrm{obs}(x,y,z,t)$). The representation is often created by fields (raster which approximate continuous surfaces). At the same level, physical processes are described as Partial Differential Equations. The uncertainty of physical observations (e.g., of location and temperature measurement) can be described by statistical properties.

Descriptions of physical processes as PDEs are perfect for combinations (Hofer and Frank 2008, 2009): processes formalized as PDE can be stacked together provided they use the same definitions for their variables.

6.3 Physical Objects

Objects are dominant in human cognition--to follow an object and its mostly non-changing properties is a much less demanding cognitive process than dealing with an ever-changing raster view. Objects have identity and properties (Shipman 1981); identity is that which is preserved across a process: when I moved from Orono, Maine to Vienna, Austria, my identity stayed the same, but many properties changed (e.g., my address). The preoccupation with data structures is a remnant of the database influence (Frank and Tamminen 1982; Frank 1983). It may be important for performance (Frank 1981), but it is certainly not fundamental. Functions that relate object identity to property values are views that integrates better with mathematics.

Object properties follow from the observed physical values and depend on their imperfections; additionally, the uncertainty in finding the boundary of an object aggravates the imperfection. In general, the imperfection follow statistical rules (e.g., Gauss's error propagation). Often physical methods to determine the properties of an object directly are devised (e.g., weighing an object on a scale). For physical objects, rules of preservation of mass or energy apply.

6.4 Social Construction

Physical objects and physical process are often socially significant. Some classic examples include (1) pieces of printed paper that serve as money (see Figure 9), or (2) affirming one's intention in a speech act to conclude a legally binding contract. Searle (1995) has coined the convenient formula "*654892253 X counts as Y in context Z*", which points out that such assignments of social meaning to physical objects are culturally, and thus context, dependent.

Figure 9: Ten euro bill (From: http://en.wikipedia.org/wiki/
File:EUR_10_obverse_%282002_issue%29.jpg)

Socially constructed objects have an identity, which is usually
separate from the identity of the underlying physical objects. Social
processes change the state of the object and may produce new
objects.

The properties of socially constructed objects are usually without
error (e.g., the ten euro bill in Figure 9 has a value of exactly ten
euro, but only in the context of the countries where this is legal
tender); similarly, a marriage ceremony is either completely
performed and valid or not at all--legally, one cannot be "ninety
percent married"! The uncertainty in a social constructed fact is
whether it is valid or not (e.g., is the bill counterfeit?). The
determination is typically a social process (e.g., legal procedures in
court resulting in a determination that it is either completely valid or
completely counterfeit).

6.5 Context

The influence of context on human perception, classification, and
encoding of observations is known, but it has resisted attempts for
formalization. It applies to the social construction of language (i.e.,
how words are related to referents (see Figure 4a). Rosch has given
substantial empirical evidence for a prototype theory for meaning
(Rosch 1973). A formalization of the prototype effects was given by
Gabora et al. (2008). It is based on quantum mechanics (i.e., a
mathematical theory; Lawden 2005) to deal with uncertainty, a
broader model than the previously attempted probabilistic ones. The
method described can be applied in a geographic situation, for
example, to explain the factual difference in what the symbol for

forest represents on a map of Greece, Austria, or Finland; it is currently not evident how to extend the approach to scale to large applications.

7. Formalism to Describe Process

The goal to expand GIS to a "dynamic description of space" can only be achieved if a suitable method to describe the processes is selected. Classic philosophy considered a world that is mostly static (with some exceptions, such as Heraclitus saying "Everything changes and nothing remains still . . . and . . . you cannot step twice into the same stream."). Logic as a formal method is perfect to describe static relations and deductions; it was the foundation for the (static) database discussion of the 1980s (Gallaire et al. 1984).

Logic is limited in what it can describe, as it does not lend itself to describe process (Guarino 1995a). It is hard to formalize temporal sequences (see McCarthy's frame problem; McCarthy 1980), despite the fact that anything formally expressible can be written in logic notation--but not in a logic notation that can be read and understood by humans.

A better approach to describe processes (or operations) formally is through functions: Universal Algebra (Whitehead 1898) defines operations that act on some domain and formalize their semantics. Universal algebra is general enough to include models of the processes of interest to geography that are changing a state into a new state. Geographic processes can be formalized as functions that transform a state of the world into a new state (i.e., the domain and the co-domain of the function is the same, a so-called endomorphism). Adding functions to observe specific aspects of the state produces formal definitions with defined semantics in the form of algebraic specifications (Frank and Kuhn 1998).

8. Conclusion

The evolution of GIS as a "repository of all possible

maps" (Chrisman 2012) to a "Geography simulator" (perhaps not exactly as envisioned by Plamen Dejanov), an evolution that models processes for analysis of the past and prediction of futures, is most likely a paradigm change (Kuhn 1962). The new paradigm of the spatial time machine (i.e., a dynamic, temporal GIS) is built around different mathematical principles--lambda calculus in lieu of predicate calculus--and some of the heated discussions of the past ("raster" vs. "vector" data structures) are discarded as technology issues, important for performance, but not fundamental.

The second paradigm change applies to semantics, now often labeled as ontology in computer science, and which is useful as a conceptualization of some part of reality (Gruber 2008; Guarino 1995b). It is common today to posit a single ontology (or even a universal ontology) and ignore the imperfections of knowledge. Accepting the unavoidable uncertainty, subjectivity, and context dependence of human knowledge, a separation of the ontology in tiers as levels of imperfection in how well it approximates a "universal, objective truth". Knowledge in each tier must be treated accordingly. This is a change in the paradigm for how semantics, taxonomies, and ontologies are dealt with in information technology, which influences GIScience.

A third paradigm change regards a move away from monolithic models (or monolithic systems) to the identification of simpler processes and methods to combine simpler parts to form complex objects and processes; the difficulty is not so much in identification and description of the simple process than in the structure of the-- hopefully generic--combination of processes. The combination methods are comparable to the grammar of natural languages, where a limited vocabulary is combined into an infinite number of meaningful sentences (de Saussure 1916).

In detail, in this article I have found fundamental principles and places where these principles are lacking:

> 1. Methodologically, GIScience should become more mathematical-formal and address in detail the grounding problem.

> 2. GIScience should focus on description of processes and

collections of related processes.

3. Generic methods for combination of complex processes from simpler process es are urgently needed.

4. The different aspects of geometry must be unified to be used in a GIS.

5. A tiered ontology separates different types of knowing, which are represented, combine and reason with imperfections differently.

The search for fundamentals reveals not only principles that are used widely in GIScience, but also fundamental topics for long-term research. Most difficult is the understanding of the interaction between physical and social realities; Chrisman's concern brings results from social science, public administration studies, etc. to GIScience. The tiered ontology, specifically tier 2 (physical objects) and tier 3 (socially constructed objects) is at the core of bringing together the physical and the social realm as connections between tier 2 and 3.

Among the fundamental principles where I find wide usage are the formal, mathematical, and usually quantitative approach; unfortunately, too much is still influenced by a static viewpoint, inherited from the past view of a GIS as a database for all potential maps. The future for GIS is as a spatial time machine!

Acknowledgment

I carry an enormous debt to the many people who have helped my thinking along. I will first mention Waldo Tobler and his colleagues from the "quantitative revolution" in geography, whom I had the pleasure to meet in person: Getis, Nystuyen, and Marble. I acknowledge the influence of Ron Abler, who, as the responsible NSF program officer, made NCGIA happen. His thinking, as expressed in the Abler, Adams, and Gould book (Abler 1971), clarified for me what geography was all about. During long discussions, my colleagues from NCGIA, the late David Simonett,

Mike Goodchild, Mike Batty, David Mark, Helen Couclelis, Dan Montello, and others shaped the intellectual program of NCGIA and influenced my own research. The work with David Mark, Max Egenhofer, and Werner Kuhn in the Las Navas meetings, as well as the talks with George Lakoff and Len Talmy must be mentioned, as they exposed my positions to their arguments (Mark 1989).

Figures 2, 4a, and 4b are from Wikipedia, the valuable reference source. I acknowledge the contribution that Wikipedia articles have made to clarify my thinking.

References

Abler, R., Adams, J. S., Gould, P., 1971. *Spatial Organization - The Geographer's View of the World*. New York: Prentice Hall.

Asperti, A., Longo, G., 1991. *Categories, Types and Structures - An Introduction to Category Theory for the Working Computer Scientist*, 1st Edition. Foundations of Computing. Cambridge, MA: The MIT Press.

Blumenthal, L. M., 1986. *A Modern View of Geometry*. Dover Publications, Inc.

Blumenthal, L. M., Menger, K., 1970. *Studies in Geometry*. A Series of Books in Mathematics. New York: W.H. Freeman and Company.

Brachmann, R., Levesque, H., Reiter, R. (Eds.), 1992. *A Spatial Logic Based on Regions and Connection*. Third International Conference on the Principles of Knowledge Representation and Reasoning. Los Altos, CA: Morgan- Kaufmann.

Bulbul, R., Frank, A., 2009a. Big integers for GIS: Testing the viability of arbitrary precision arithmetic for gis geometry. In:

Bulbul, R., Frank, A. U., 2009b. AHD: The alternate hierarchical decomposition of non-convex polytopes (generalization of a convex polytope based spatial data model). In: 17th International Conference on Geoinformatics. Fairfax, USA, 12-14August2009.

Bulbul, R., Frank, A. U., 2009c. AHD: the alternate hierarchical decomposition of non-convex polytopes (generalization of a convex polytope based spatial data model). In: 17th International Conference on Geoinformatics. Vienna: IEEE.

Chrisman, N., 2012. A deflationary approach to fundamental principles in GIScience. In: Harvey F (ed.) this volume.

Chrisman, N. R., 1975. Topological Information Systems for Geographic Representation. Unpublished Paper, Harvard University, Lab for Computer Graphics.

de Saussure, F., 1995 (1916). *Cours de linguistique générale*. Paris: Payot & Rivages.

Eco, U., 1976. *A Theory of Semiotics. Advances in Semiotics*. Indianapolis: Indiana University Press.

Egenhofer, M., Dube, M., 2009. Topological relations from metric refinements. In: Proceedings of the 17th ACM SIGSPATIAL International Conference on Advances in Geographic Information Systems. ACM, pp. 158-167.

Egenhofer, M. J., Franzosa, R. D., 1991. Point-set topological spatial relations. *International Journal of Geographical Information Systems* 5(2), 161-174.

Frank, A., 1982. Datenstrukturen für Landinformationssysteme - semantische, topologische und räumliche Beziehungen in Daten der Geo-wissenschaften. Ph.D. Thesis. ETH-Zürich,

Zürich, Switzerland.

Frank, A., 1988. Requirements for a database management system for a GIS. *Photogrammetric Engineering and Remote Sensing*. 54(11), 1557–1564.

Frank, A., 1998. GIS for Politics. *GIS Planet*. 98: 9–11.

Frank, A. U., 1981. Application of DBMS to land information systems. Seventh International Conference on Very Large Data Bases VLDB. Cannes, France, September 1981.

Frank, A. U., 1990. Spatial concepts, geometric data models and data structures. GIS Design Models and Functionality. Midlands Regional Research Laboratory, University of Leicester.

Frank, A. U., 2001. Tiers of ontology and consistency constraints in Geographic Information Systems. *International Journal of Geographic Information Science*, 15: 667-678.

Frank, A., 2007. Data quality ontology: An ontology for imperfect knowledge. In: Proceedings of the 8th international conference on Spatial Information Theory. 406–420. Berlin: Springer-Verlag.

Frank, A. U., 2008. Analysis of dependence of decision quality on data quality. *Journal of Geographical Systems* 10 (1), 71–88.

Frank, A. U., Kuhn, W., 1998. "A Specification Language for Interoperable GIS." In Interoperating Geographic Information Systems. 123-132. Berlin: Springer Verlag.

Frank, A. U., Tamminen, M., 1982. Management of spatially referenced data. In *Land Information at the Local Level*. Department of Surveying Engineering, 330–353. Orono: University of Maine at Orono.

Frank, A. U., Volta, G. S., McGranaghan, M., 1997. Formalization of families of categorical coverages. *International Journal of*

Geographic Information Systems 11(3):215–231.

Gabora, L., Rosch, E., Aerts, D., 2008. Toward an ecological theory of concepts. *Ecological Psychology*, 20:84–116.

Gallaire, H., Minker, J., Nicolas, J.-M., 1984. Logic and databases: A deductive approach. ACM Computing Surveys (CSUR) 16 (2), 153–184.

Galton, A., 2008. Processes and events. In: S. Shekar, H. Xiong. (Ed.), Encyclopedia of GIS. Berlin: Springer.

Golledge, R. G., 2008. Behavioral geography and the theoretical/ quantitative revolution. *Geographical Analysis* 40(3):239–257.

Goodchild, M., 1992. Geographical data modeling. *Computers and Geosciences* 18(4):401–408.

Goodchild, M., Yuan, M., Cova, T., 2007. Towards a general theory of geographic representation in GIS. *International Journal of Geographical Information Science* 21(3):239–260.

Gruber, T., 2008. Ontology. In: *Encyclopedia of Database Systems*. Berlin: Springer-Verlag.

Guarino, N., 1995a. Formal ontology, conceptual analysis and knowledge representation. *International Journal of Human Computer Studies* 43(5):625–640.

Guarino, N., 1995b. Formal ontology, conceptual analysis and knowledge representation. *International Journal of Human and Computer Studies*. Special Issue on Formal Ontology, Conceptual Analysis and Knowledge Representation. 43:5-6.

Hofer, B., Frank, A., 2008. Toward a method to generally describe physical spatial processes. Headway in Spatial Data Handling, 217–232. Berlin: Springer Verlag.

Hofer, B., Frank, A., 2009. Composing models of geographic

physical processes. In: Spatial Information Theory, 421–435. COSIT'09 Proceedings of the 9th international conference on Spatial information theory. 421–435. Berlin: Springer Verlag.

Hofstadter, D. R., 1979. *Gödel, Escher, Bach: An Eternal Golden Braid*. Vintage Books: New York.

Karimipour, F., Delavar, M., Frank, A. U., 2008. A mathematical tool to extend 2D spatial operations. In: *Computational Science and Its Applications - ICCSA 2008*, LNCS 5072 /Part 1, edited by Gervasi, O., Murgante, B., Laganà, A., Taniar, D., Mun, Y., Gavrilova, M., 153–164. Heidelberg: Springer.

Karimipour, F., Delavar, M., Frank, A. U., 2009. An algebraic approach to extend spatial operations to moving objects. *World Applied Sciences Journal* 6(10) 1377-1383.

Kuhn, T., 1962. *The Structure of Scientific Revolutions*. Chicago: University of Chicago Press.

Kuhn, T. S., 1970. *The Structure of Scientific Revolutions*, Vol. 2(2) of International Encyclopedia of Unified Science. 2nd Edition. Chicago: The University of Chicago Press.

Lakoff, G., 1987. *Women, Fire, and Dangerous Things: What Categories Reveal About the Mind*. Chicago: University of Chicago Press.

Lakoff, G., Johnson, M., 1980. *Metaphors We Live By*. Chicago: University of Chicago Press.

Lakoff, G., Nuñez, R. E., 2000. *Where Mathematics Comes From - How the Embodied Mind Brings Mathematics into Being*. New York: Basic Books.

Lawden, D. F., 2005. *The Mathematical Principles of Quantum Mechanics*. New York: Dover Publications, Inc.

MacLane, S., Birkhoff, G., 1991. *Algebra Third Edition*. London:

AMS Chelsea Publishing.

Mark, D. M., Frank, A. U., 1989. Concepts of space and spatial language. Auto-Carto 9. ASPRS & ACSM, pp. 538–556. Baltimore, MD: 2-9April2009.

McCarthy, J., 1980. Circumscription - a form of non-monotonic reasoning. *Artificial Intelligence* 13:27–39.

Navratil, G., Harnoncourt, M., 2004. geotalk: eine raum-zeit-kommunikationsplattform. *CORP*, Vienna, Austria.

Ogden, C., Richards, I., 1923 (1989). *The Meaning of Meaning*. New York: Harcourt, Brace, Jovanovich, Inc.

Popper, K. R., 1984. *Logik der Forschung*. 8th Edition. Vol. 4 of Die Einheit der Gesellschaftswissenschaften. Tübingen, Germany: J. C. B. Mohr.

Randell, D.A., Cui, Z., Cohn, A.Brachmann, R., Levesque, H., Reiter, R. (Eds.), 1992. A Spatial Logic Based on Regions and Connection. In: Brachmann, R., Levesque, H., Reiter, R. (Eds.), *Third International Conference on the Principles of Knowledge Representation and Reasoning*. Los Altos, CA: Morgan- Kaufmann.

Raubal, M., 2001. Agent-based simulation of human wayfinding: A perceptual model for unfamiliar buildings. Ph.D. thesis. Technical University of Vienna.

Reitsma, F., Albrecht, J., 2005. Implementing a new data model for simulating processes. *International Journal of Geographical Information Science* 19(10): 1073–1090.

Rizzolatti, G., Craighero, L., 2004. The mirror-neuron system. *Annual Review of Neuroscience* 27:169–192.

Rosch, E., 1973. Natural categories. *Cognitive Psychology* 4,

328-350.

Scheider, S., Janowicz, K., Kuhn, W., 2009. Grounding geographic categories in the meaningful environment. COSIT'09 Proceedings of the 9th international conference on Spatial information theory. 69-87. Berlin: Springer Verlag.

Searle, J., 1976. A classification of illocutionary acts. *Language in society* 5 (1), 1-23.

Searle, J. R., 1995. *The Construction of Social Reality*. The Free Press.

Shipman, D. W., 1981. The functional data model and the data language duplex. ACM Transactions on Database Systems 6 (March).

Simon, H. A., 1997. *Administrative Behavior: A Study of Decision-Making Process in Administrative Organizations*, 4th Edition. The Free Press.

Tobler, W. R., 1976. Analytical cartography. *The American Cartographer* 3 (1), 21-31.

Tomlin, C. D., 1983. Digital cartographic modeling techniques in environmental planning. Ph.D. Thesis. Princeton, NJ: Yale University.

Treiblmayr, M., Scheider, S., Krüger, A., von der Linden, M., 2012. Integrating GI with non-GI services - showcasing interoperability in a heterogeneous service-oriented architecture. *Geoinformatica*, 16(1) 207-220

Ullman, J. D., 1988. *Principles of Database and Knowledgebase Systems*. Vol. 1 of Principles of Computer Science Series. New York: Computer Science Press.

Wells, H., 1895 (1971). *The Time Machine: An Invention*.

Cambridge, MA: R. Bentley.

Whitehead, A., 1898. *A Treatise on Universal Algebra*. Cambridge: Cambridge University Press.

Wierzbicka, A., 1996. *Semantics - Primes and Universals*. Oxford: Oxford University Press.

A deflationary approach to fundamental principles in GIScience

Nicholas Chrisman
Université Laval
nicholas.chrisman@geoide.ulaval.ca
(From January 2013: RMIT University;
nicholas.chrisman@rmit.edu.au)

1. Background

While the practice of mapping has ancient, even prehistoric, roots, the past fifty years have seen increased emphasis on the sciences of geographic information. A key element is moving from the fixation with the specific constraints of the mapped product (the graphic artifact) to re-centering attention on databases as the resources for constructing all potential maps, and the GIS as the basis for all models of process of change. There is an early indication of this approach enunciated in a short (three-page) article by John Sherman and Waldo Tobler in Professional Geographer (Sherman and Tobler 1957; Chrisman 1997a). This was followed by a work on the promise of digital technology (Tobler 1959). Perhaps one of the clearest articulations in the rethinking of cartography was Board's (1967) "Maps as Models".

The first textbook for teaching GIS adopted the title *Principles of Geographical Information Systems for Land Resources Assessment* (Burrough 1986), thereby adopting the idea of a set of basic principles to apply to the developing GIS scene. A clear case of this move is evident in Andrew Frank's (1987) treatment of overlay processing, in which he argues for a "conceptual approach" (17) rather than one based on implementations. Frank's final sentence set the agenda quite clearly: "The separation into a few relatively simple concepts can benefit the design of the user interface and would result in systems which are easier to learn and easier to use" (Frank 1987, 29-30). Viewed from twenty-four years later, this tendency persists, despite the evident lack of impact on the feature-laden user interfaces now in use. In more recent years, this viewpoint is so commonplace that it would be fruitless to cite all instances. Goodchild and Sui, in various articles, have offered reviews of the subject built on the metaphor of the Tower of Babel and the urge for a common unifying language (Goodchild 1992; Sui 1999; Sui and Goodchild 2001). This chapter was written in parallel with Frank (2012) as a joint reflection on the issues of fundamental principles.

2. Are there fundamental concepts in GIScience?

This essay derives from a long engagement with the subject, and a long engagement in debating different approaches with colleagues over forty years. It takes some explaining to establish what we have been debating. At first glance, of course there are fundamental principles in GIScience. If there is any science in what we do, we all must understand some of the basic elements to be able to work together. But, such a statement, in its sweeping form, raises the crucial issues. Who are the "we", and how do we so universally share some common understandings?

In 1987, right after Andrew Frank's presentation at AUTO-CARTO 8 cited above, I presented under the title "Fundamental Principles of GIS" (an essay later published under a more descriptive [and less grandiose] title

(Chrisman, 1987)). That year signaled twenty years since the first publications using the GIS term, providing an occasion for reflection just as much as the fifty-year signpost that occasions this event. My 1987 essay started with a concern to address "fundamental" principles, particularly related to the choice of data model--an issue that was still current at the time. By the end of the first column of text, I had turned the issue from the fundamentals of mathematics to the "deep issues of why we collect and process geographic information" (Chrisman 1987, 1367). The 1987 text made reference to a paper from ten years earlier in which I had argued that two geographic data structures (raster and vector) were so dissimilar that they were incommensurate (Chrisman 1978). The paper then tried to dethrone the classic communications model that posits messages passing unfiltered through channels (a theme that returned in Poore and Chrisman 2006).

In many respects, I shared the viewpoint of Andrew Frank (rearticulated in Frank 2012) that we needed to divorce ourselves from specific implementations to discuss fundamental issues on some conceptual plane. My argument in 1987 turned toward the design of systems based on social goals, a direction I have attempted to refine over the decades (Chrisman 2002; Harvey and Chrisman 2004). Where Frank (1987) supported a "normalized" view of databases, the social analysis in my 1987 essay required a more diffuse decentralized engagement between actors with roles of custodians, validated by mandates and other social goals (specifically equity over cost-savings). By 2012, Frank (2012) argues that our GIScience is overly influenced by a "database" static view, and he proposes a "process" viewpoint. This essay will explore an alternative approach to fundamental principles, leading to a different approach toward process as well.

The 1987 engagement was just one episode in the debate, but one that problematized the "universality" of pronouncements about principles. The theme did not die out. In a co-authored editorial, Peter Burrough and Andrew Frank (1995) posed the rhetorical question: "are current GIS truly generic?" Their complex argument covered much of philosophy and cognition, with detours to cite Monty Python. The complex argument arrived at a multi-dimensional scaling (three dimensions to compress five "aspects" located by some ill-defined subjective 0 to 1 scale measurements) in which to situate the various viewpoints of schools of thought in the GIS arena (Burrough and Frank 1995, 113). The two authors concluded that the distinct paradigms are so different that a single generic solution is hard to imagine; the viewpoint of each co-author must be taken into consideration, as always.

Andrew Frank (2001) introduced a series of "tiers" in what he termed ontology, but that he accepts extends to include issues of a more epistemological flavor. In fact, Frank introduces a different approach to the philosophy of science at each tier, from a radical realism at the base level to a subjective social constructivism at the cognitive level. At each tier in his framework, Frank changes the definition of "fundamental", an approach that is problematic and ends up with not much more than positional statements from the viewpoint of various actors. In this paper, I will try to provide an argument for abandoning this concept of tiers completely.

In a similar vein, I revisited my 1987 article in a paper presented at GISRUK in 2001 (Chrisman 2002). I criticized my earlier work as overly structuralist, in that it placed too much emphasis on historically embedded social and institutional entities, not leaving much room for agency to modify the structures. I had become uncomfortable with the implicit "superorganic" entities that seemed to live on their own "tier" without reference to actual people. This is a theme of increased interest recently. The 2001 paper includes a much richer connection to the field of Science and Technology Studies (STS), a field that had been acknowledged in a minor way through the use of terms like

"paradigm" (often without the citation to Kuhn (1970).
Beyond the over-used term "paradigm", the paper focused
on the issue of technological determinism and how the user
is configured to fit the technology, and not necessarily the
other way around. The paper ends with an emphasis on the
division of knowledge, something that provides an
alternative to Frank's tiers (Frank 2001, 2012). Software
developers are often trying to work inside an existing
definition of who-knows-what, rather than working in a
cognitive paradigm from Artificial Intelligence.
Consequently, the easy division between Society and GIS
becomes more and more difficult to defend or detect.

This review has concentrated on the works of Andrew
Frank and myself not because we are the best at articulating
the question, but more as a sample to be connected to other
work. Frank's tiers can be seen in even more elaborate
development in Raper's (2000) progression through layers
of philosophy of science. Similarly, the questioning about
the truth statements about the science of GIScience relates
to the questioning of media (Sui 1999; Sui and Goodchild
2001; Harvey and Chrisman 2004).

In the discourse of the GIS field, the issue of "fundamental
principles" has remained something to debate and use as a
springboard for other issues of importance. It will not go
away. Perhaps the most useful question was posed by
Tobler (1976) in terms of the half-life of the concepts in his
course on analytical cartography. (Frank 2012) uses this as
the introduction to his article.) Tobler expressed the desire
that half the concepts would still be valid twenty years
later. In my personal experiment, I found that Tobler was
modest in his claim; about sixty percent of his course
content was valuable twenty-six years later (Chrisman
2001). Of course, the rate of decay in the various isotopes
of the course was uneven. Some elements were more
directly linked to the primitive equipment of the time;
others dealt with already long-standing mathematical
findings. The off-the-cuff prediction of a wrist-watch

positioning system was one of the elements validated through the course of technological events.

These empirical findings provide a start to deflate claims about abstract universals in GIScience. Claims for the enduring persistence of fundamental principles are in fact subject to empirical validation; it just takes time. Examination of course curricula may prove the clearest demonstration, since the time available for a course is essentially a constant. While the body of knowledge may expand, the instructor must prune back the growing bush to keep the course coherent. The process of leaving something out, forgetting an element judged important in the past, is a crucial act in the progress of science. Bowker (2005) and others in STS have begun to study these memory practices in a more general way. Frank (2012) refers to Popper on falsification of theories and what is excluded. This focus can be extended to what we forget to explain to our students about the phylogeny of our body of knowledge.

3. The deflationary turn

One problem with fundamental principles is that they can be asserted in a way that denies debate. If they are strictly fundamental, they must also be universal, for all time, and self-evident. This naïve Universalist claim was particularly apparent in an earlier era of "social physics" with statements about the rank-size rule and the "law of least effort" (Zipf 1949), but it persists in many forums at least in a tacit form. Frank (2012) has a kind of nostalgic attraction to timeless science, a foundation that is immune from debate. He places mathematics in this category, though there is plenty of evidence to suggest that the history of mathematics is far from unilinear (Boyer and Merzbach 2011). Nearly 2000 years ago, Sixtus Empiricus posed a paradox for the dominant Stoic school of the era (Barrow 1992, 277) that is similar to the anti-essentialist argument that I propose in this essay. Plato positions mathematical truth on some higher plane, remote from human frailties, and therein lies the inconsistency (how then do we gain access to this higher plane of existence?). A more recent lesson from the history of mathematics is that Hilbert's formalist agenda must confront Gödel's demonstration that complex systems necessarily include statements that cannot be proven inside the closed world of formalism (for an application to the agenda of Artificial Intelligence, see Penrose 1989). The odd part here is that both Gödel and Penrose are ardent Platonists. For me, the Platonism behind the formalist agenda introduces immaterial entities immune from observation. I do not see the need to build a structure that depends on so much metaphysics. As an alternative, some would argue that mathematics is not "discovered" in some abstract timeless truth, but "constructed" in a contingent sequence that depends on the personalities involved, their time and place (Barrow 1992, 265ff). However, the history of mathematics is not the issue here.

Frank (2012, 2) argues for a "limited" universalism based on the limitations of what can be established by the games played with symbols without reference to the world. Frank (2012, 3) also invokes Popper on the incremental advances of science, but then moves quickly to assert that mathematical truth is "nearly timeless" along with a reconfirmation of formalism as a means to truth. Limited or not, Frank remains tied to a universalist stance. Universalism is not about determinism, but about how certain assertions apply to all places and times. Frank and many of his colleagues have sought solace in mathematical formalism in the hopes that their work will stand some test of time. In most cases, this means a deliberate separation from what they see as social issues. Frank talks about "grounding" as a means of attaching formalism to the world, with some hope of a one-to-one correspondence that requires a lot of work to maintain. I find this stance hard to explain.

As an alternative, I wish to bring in an approach from the philosophy of science that addresses the inconsistencies that Frank catalogs at the different tiers of ontology, and explains the grounding process more as a two-way feedback. Rather than isolating the "social" component to the higher levels, far away from the inescapable physical fact, I offer a coherent approach that seeks to avoid the division into tiers.

My proposed approach derives from a paper that Sergio Sismondo and I published in *Philosophy of Science* (Sismondo and Chrisman 2001). The paper developed an issue in that field concerning the correspondence between scientific theories and the world, through the observation that much of this literature uses the map as a metaphor to talk about theories. Philosophers of science, much like the folk tale about the blindfolded observation of an elephant, obtain different readings through the map metaphor. Robinson and Petchenik (1976) had observed much the same divergences in the use of the map metaphor. For Sismondo and me, the different interpretations of maps seemed totally consistent. Maps serve different functions in different settings; sometimes they are best seen as realist, other times as instrumental, and in other cases constructed.

By adopting a stance of "deflationary realism", Sismondo argues that the divergent examples all make sense if one keeps the claims of explanation modest. The deflationary approach derives from what Arthur Fine (1986) called a "Natural Ontological Attitude" (NOA). The naturalness comes by abjuring the extra additives imposed by more extreme versions of realism and anti-realism. NOA stands on two supports: anti-essentialist and anti-interpretive, with an injunction to leave all metaphysical baggage behind.

Essentialism is the tendency or orientation to assert the "fundamental" nature of certain elements (like fundamental principles). This tendency exists in all fields, and GIScience is not immune. Frank's observation of the different tiers and his explanation of imperfect knowledge show an engagement with the inconsistencies of essentialism. We cannot stick to one tier or another; our knowledge is never totally reliable. Geographic representations are at times instrumental, at times not. They are often rock-solid "facts", and at other times quite subject to interpretation by different actors. Reduced forms of information may be much more "useful" than the mass of facts behind them.

Frank (2012, 18) uses an illustration of a ten euro note to introduce "social construction". This kind of socially sanctioned value is not surprising in any way. Money, particularly in modern paper or virtual form, is a matter of trust and social institutions, and a long distance from "hard facts". Frank brings in "context" as a form of explanation. Yet, context is a very slippery concept, often used ex-post to tell just-so stories. This is where a deflationary account helps restrain the table thumping. A ten-euro note is worth ten euro exactly because of the supporting infrastructure of banks, international agreements, and social trust. It is hard to extract the value of the euro from all the work behind the scenes to make it appear so inherent and effortless (see Latour 1999 for some other examples). Context is not an entity that can be sensed in the world in any concrete way, rather it is an explanation after the fact of what was important to know. The concept of context, despite its currency in computer science circles, has little explanatory value in this kind of debate. Latour *et al* (2012) recently took the provocative stance that there is no need to postulate "superorganic" entities like anthills, nations, or societies. By adopting data-mining approaches, there is no need to aggregate upwards. This recent work is a part of the anti-essentialist thread adopted by this paper, since it avoids predefining what exists. Latour (2012) also argues that "the whole is less than the sum of the parts", in opposition to Frank's (2012, 8) assertion that complexity emerges from simple atomic objects. I do not have the space here to review or evaluate this confrontation, only the space to suggest that a debate still persists.

Ten-euro notes (and the various interpretations of monads and complexity theory) are not really the subject matter of our GIScience discourse. Let us take an example of much more direct pertinence: the bedrock of our GIS enterprise, our geographic coordinates. These measurements appear to be firmly mathematical in their representation, yet they derive from an architecture of assumptions and treatments that are historically bound and thus contingent rather than fundamental. We can assert, for example, that a geodetic datum is "socially constructed" to acknowledge the careful work of standards committees that sat for years to bring World Geodetic Standards 1984 (WGS) into being. Acknowledging this necessary work does not mean to bring it into disrepute as arguable. The deflationary stance tries to avoid jumping to value statements. As Hacking (1999) observed, the term "socially constructed" is often used in a sense of ridicule or criticism, as we can observe in Harley's (1989) critique of maps as political messages. Here, the deflationary stance allows us to simply record and acknowledge the combination of mathematics and organizational logics that uphold the WGS. They are neither pure mathematics nor corrupt human institutions, but rather a mix of human agency and mathematical models through and through.

Both Andrew Frank and I have supervised PhD students whose work explored the epistemological underpinnings of simple assertions like that coordinates for define property boundaries. Frank (2012) cites his student Buyong (1992), while I would cite my student Karnes (1995) in setting out a pluralistic means to adjudicate the best use of the historical record of measurements at any given time. These PhD dissertations are examples that argue against an "essential" truth in one source over another.

In terms of interpretation, Fine's NOA begins with a basic level of agreement that the best-established claims are sufficiently justified. It is "natural" (or unproblematic) to accept them as "true". NOA resists any attempt to add other accounts: correspondence, pragmatic, instrumentalist, or conventionalist. Thus, Fine has a simple approach to "truth"--statements that we have good evidence to support. Some "table-thumping" realist may insist that electrons are really real, and Fine can calmly agree that we have sufficient evidence; no need to get worked up about it. Sismondo argues that Fine runs into trouble around here because his anti-essentialism conflicts with his anti-interpretivism. No matter the fine points, we can still retain the approach of not granting extravagant value to statements that appear to have sufficient evidence to support them.

Sismondo and Chrisman (2001) bring in various examples of maps to demonstrate where Fine's NOA runs into trouble. Understanding abstract symbol systems such as maps and models requires some interpretation of a metaphysical sort. One example is to consider the use of the Mercator projection for nautical charts. This projection is a perfectly reasonable choice to make certain operations easy (compass bearings lead to straight lines on the chart), at a certain cost (distances vary by latitude). Yet, when some diplomats meet to determine nautical boundaries between countries, they will not find much other than the nautical chart for their deliberations. The geometric midpoint between two coasts may not appear to be a fair solution when drawn on the chart. Many maritime boundaries are thereby located with much less equity than the actors thought they would exhibit (Lathrop 1997). Therefore, the subsequent map user needs to understand the interpretations made in the original user scenario, and not import any preconceived notions about geometry. The affordances of the Mercator projection have to be used inside a well-defined practice, otherwise it is easy to mislead on properties of distance or area. Some measure of interpretation is required.

This philosophical stance implies a very restrained, hence deflationary, level of metaphysics, but the kind that the expert analyst must learn to make sense of abstractions. In day-to-day work, many practitioners in GIScience adopt a basic level of deflation without using the label.

4. Applying deflationary analysis to Tobler's Law

To demonstrate the utility of the deflationary stance, I will proceed to consider what has been termed "Tobler's First Law of Geography" (Tobler 2004; Miller 2004; Sui 2004). This "Law" states: "Everything is related to everything else, but near things are more related than distant things". (This statement was announced by Tobler (1970) as the "first law of geography", but attributed under his own name only more recently.) As laws go, this one is loosely formulated and without concrete predictions. As Tobler (2004, 309) points out, a rather similar formulation was made by the statistician Fisher in 1935. Hecht and Moxley (2009) have presented what they term evidence to support the assertion, based on an analysis of Wikipedia entries. The deflationary stance finds this all unremarkable. Tobler's Law (or indeed Fisher's Law) might well have substantial evidence to support them, so why not treat them as "true"?

A formalist might feel that a "real" law has to have clearly defined terms, not just "things" and "relationships". And, of course, there are those who insist on laws with mathematical predictions that can be falsified or at least potentially disproved. Tobler's Law may be a last weak restatement of the social physics movement (such as Zipf 1949) that tried to specify the power function for distance decay. From certain studies, we can ascertain if the distance between social interactions actually declines with the inverse square of distance or not. Certain geographers (such as Barnes 1991) have criticized this movement with quite complex arguments that I will not reproduce in this essay. Barnes in his turn makes a case for a different interpretation of the role of science, one based on a different epistemology. The conflict on the geography front of the Science Wars is perhaps as irreducibly futile as elsewhere. With a deflationary stance, the amount of influence of the time and place in which some work was done is just another interpretation to take into account.

This essay will examine a few of the commentaries offered on the subject of Tobler's First Law (TFL) in a forum edited by Sui (2004) in the *Annals of the AAG*. The deflationary stance offers a means to balance the irreconcilable viewpoints and provides a means to address fundamental principles. Most importantly, Barnes (2004) attempts to offer an anti-law proposition based on what he terms "anti-philosophy of science", namely science studies. I do not see any such opposition. The deflationary stance is developed by philosophers of science with substantial grounding in the discourse. Beyond Fine (1986), the deflationary stance relates to Giere's (1999) "Science without Laws" as well as various works of Hacking (1999), Feyerabend (1975) and others. It is quite correct that this viewpoint is not the approach from the mid-twentieth century (such as Carnap 1966). However, various arguments have deep roots, and it is hard to characterize another discipline in a short space. Barnes seeks to reject outright the use of the term law. Tobler (2004, 304-305) responds by citing the fallibility of philosophers, and arguing for greater faith in empirical results, adopting Richard Feynman's more lax views on what may be better termed models than laws. To each of these arguments, the deflationary stance provides a place of balance in a surprisingly taut debate.

Goodchild's (2004) contribution as discussant in the above debate takes a version of the deflationary approach. He argues that the use of the term "law" or principle or theory is not of great importance. What matters more is the utility of the statement in teaching and application. But, deep down, Goodchild retains his training in physics and looks for the "universal, true, and eminently useful" (2004, 303) in the archetype Boyle's Law. Like Barnes, I have read Shapin and Shafer's (1985) historical account of Boyle's experiments. It provides a clear study of the relation of the scientist to his or her time and place. Yet, there is room for a measure of realism here. However Boyle (or Newton or Tobler) was influenced by his social and historical setting, something portable remains. This "immutable mobile", as Latour (1993) terms it, is invariant as it is translated from one use to another. If Boyle held hierarchical and aristocratic views of society, it certainly had an influence on his methods and how he construed "proof". His Law, however, can be proved by other means to suit whatever taste. It makes sense to accept that gasses expand to fill a space, following a specific mathematical formulation. This part is indeed portable. The deflationary stance withholds the judgment about universality, which is more a result of the test of time than something we can determine here and now.

5. Dealing with process

Frank (2012) argues for a change in paradigm from the view conditioned by a static database towards a more dynamic view of process through time. On the surface, this sounds a bit inconsistent with the view that principles are timeless. Yet, of course, the urge to deal with the dynamics of the world system is of long standing. Frank's treatment of functions, functors, and other constructions serves to demonstrate how elements of a formal logic can be combined to model complex processes. I share Frank's determination to orient the practitioners of GIScience to pay more attention to history, time, and process (Chrisman 1997b; Poore and Chrisman 2006). We do not agree (yet) on the means to this end.

Frank proposes a paradigm of a "spatial time machine" as the start of a list of paradigm shifts that he foresees. The tiered ontology divisions remain a central part of this conception, so our views remain divided. My concerns are not specifically about the role of social science or public administration (as portrayed by Frank on page 20), but on a more philosophical stance of anti-essentialism. I understand the urge to create simplified "objects" that respond to limited, tightly defined rules. I wrote programs myself, and I know how one creates little logical worlds isolated from everything else. I also learned that that formalism doesn't buy me anything in the world outside. If our models fail to represent the world, they are simply logic games of limited value.

Invoking H.G. Wells's *The Time Machine* does not align our science more closely with fundamentals. The thought experiment of dropping a current scientist into another time is perhaps fruitful in demonstrating how hard it might be to make a convincing demonstration to the residents of a different era. Our massive stores of "big data" would be hard to explain by hand-waving to the scribes of an Egyptian pharaoh. Piles of papyrus do not afford much text mining. Similarly, a future scholar may dimly remember the era when we were impressed by terabytes and 140-character messages.

The process of greater interest is the process of forgetting, of how a discipline prunes back all of the acquired details to see certain clear fundamentals that persist over decades and centuries. Our geometrical principles were developed in that Egyptian setting, and most of our property surveying would be explainable to a time machine visitor from that era. Of course, the GPS equipment would appear to be magic, though it embeds the same-old triangles. In these cases, we can be fairly sure that we are close to fundamental principles. The logic is historical and empirical, not requiring any metaphysics.

In his conclusion, Frank (2012) expects that his tiers of physical objects and social-construction can become connected, perhaps through some emergent properties. My naturalist impulse asserts that they were never disconnected, and that any order imposed is arbitrary and unproven. Latour (1999, 141) extends the work of Whitehead to explain how the relations between humans and non-humans (Frank's objects) is much more symmetrical and undecided. The more recent work by Latour *et al* (2012) on social networks and data mining are particularly pertinent in showing a way around the ontological tiers of separation. Latour contends that "the whole is less than the sum of the parts", in his usual counter-intuitive manner. Basically, he adopts an anti-essentialist (anti-Platonist) argument that social complexity does not belong in the superorganic, but in each person. These arguments are much more convincing to me. It will take time to tell if Frank's views and mine are so dramatically different, or if they have converged in all but their surface formulation.

6. Starting a list of fundamental principles

A chapter such as this one should perhaps not end without providing some guidance on fundamental principles drawing on the deflationary stance, anti-essentialism, and anti-interpretativism. To some extent, adhering to this perspective, it is premature, even illusory, to expect to have a single short list of fundamentals for all time. Like items in the curriculum of a course, the research agenda will change as the pressures on the field change and the world around us shifts. The deflationary approach can orient the development of principles in a manner that avoids the pitfalls of universalism and essential truths. More importantly, this approach can emphasize the practical utility of these principles while bringing a measure of modesty to the debates about principles.

For right now, in closing, I would propose a few samples of applying deflationary approaches coupled with anti-essentialism to the development of principles, rather than attempting to be exhaustive or canonical. The first would insist that value (in an information system) derives strictly from use. This denies the often-inflated claims of some inherent value that resides in the database.

Second, I would suggest leaving the Cartesian world behind and embracing the spherical (or better yet ellipsoidal) world as it is. There are too many false conclusions drawn and stupid measurements made when geographic software, built for projected Cartesian coordinates in a local setting, is applied at the global scale. For example, there are global databases developed with raster technology applied to degrees (so called "square degrees"). There is nothing square about them; they are not homogeneous in size or in neighborhood relationships. However, significant communities of scholars (in highly funded circumstances) have convinced themselves that this data representation makes sense. Equally, we find silly results shown for "distances" calculated to millimetric precision using entirely inappropriate algorithms on the Plat Carée projection (guilty parties not cited out of tact). Each of these flaws comes not from some tiered ontology, but from oversights and laziness on the part of system designers. The fundamental principle is that we need to respect the shape of the Earth and not imagine that our models are so important that they overrule reality.

Overall, these "fundamentals" are perhaps too reactive to errors in others. Unlike Tolber's Laws, they attempt to avoid folly rather than to distill wisdom. So be it. It may take some time to develop a set of positive fundamentals. I will leave that exercise for further research.

7. Conclusion

A generally deflationary stance towards claims of grand universality is a useful step in toning down the rhetoric in the debates over fundamental principles. With this viewpoint, we can agree that there might be some fundamental concepts that work in many settings. These useful models, such as Tobler's First Law, should form a part of instruction. However, any claim that they are timelessly universal does not seem to be of great value or importance. As a part of this stance, the anti-essentialist element is particularly crucial to deal with the current tendencies on the formalist side of GIScience. The anti-interpretative element will take additional effort to elaborate in a way that supports the pragmatic goals of GIScience in the world. The tentative fundamental principles advanced in this chapter will need some reflection and evaluation before they can be used as a guide for coursework and orienting the research enterprise.

Acknowledgements

This chapter reposes on a long process of becoming. It was supported by grants from the Social Science Research Council (Canada) and prior support by the National Science Foundation (USA). In particular, I acknowledge the discussions with ex-students and colleagues (particularly Sergio Sismondo), though this particular essay is my personal responsibility.

References

Barnes, T.J. 1991. Metaphors and Conversations in Economic Geography: Richard Rorty and the Gravity Model. *Geografiska Annaler. Series B, Human Geography*, 73(2) 111-120.

Barnes, T.J. 2004. A paper related to everything but more related to local things, *Annals of the AAG*, 94(2) 278-283.

Barrow, J.D. 1992. *Pi in the Sky: Counting, Thinking and Being*. Oxford: Oxford University Press.

Board, C. 1967. Maps as models, In: Haggett P. and Chorley R., eds. *Models in Geography*. London: Methuen. Ch. 16 pp 671-720.

Bowker, G.C. 2005. *Memory practices in the sciences*. Cambridge MA: MIT Press.

Boyer, C.B. and Merzbach, U., 2011. A History of Mathematics. Third edition, Hoboken NJ: Wiley.

Burrough, P. A. 1986. Principles of Geographical Information Systems for Land Resource Assessment. Oxford: Clarendon Press.

Burrough, P.A. and Frank, A.U. 1995. Concepts and paradigms in spatial information: are current geographical information systems truly generic? *International Journal of Geographical Information Systems*, 9(2), 101-116.

Buyong, T. 1992. Measurement-based multi-purpose cadastral systems. PhD thesis, University of Maine, Orono.

Carnap, R. 1966. *Philosophical foundations of physics; an introduction to the philosophy of science*. New York: Basic Books.

Chrisman, N. R. 1975. Topological data structures for geographic representation. Proceedings AUTO–CARTO II, 1, 346–351.

Chrisman, N.R. 1978. Concepts of space as a guide to cartographic data structures. In: Dutton, ed. Harvard Papers on Geographic Information Systems. Reading MA: Addison Wesley, vol. 5.

Chrisman, N. R. 1987. Design of information systems based on social and cultural goals. *Photogrammetric Engineering and Remote Sensing*, 53, 1367–1370.

Chrisman, N.R. 1997a, John Sherman and the Origin of GIS. *Cartographic Perspectives*, (27) 8-13.

Chrisman, N.R.., 1997b, Beyond the snapshot: Changing the approach to change, error and process, In: Egenhofer, M. and Golledge, R. eds. *Spatial and Temporal Reasoning in*

Geographic Information Systems, Oxford: Oxford Univ. Press.

Chrisman, N.R. 1999. A transformational approach to GIS operations. *International Journal of Geographical Information Science*, 13(7) 617–37.

Chrisman, N.R. 2001. Analytical cartography course materials (online). http://chrisman.scg.ulaval.ca/Geog_465.html; Accessed 29 January 2012.

Chrisman, N.R. 2002. Revisiting Fundamental Principles. In: Kidner, Higgs and White, eds. *Innovations in GIS*. London: Taylor & Francis, Chapter 2, p. 9-18.

Fine, A. 1986. Unnatural attitudes: Realist and instrumentalist attachments to science. *Mind*, 95, 149-179.

Feyerabend, P. A. 1975. Against method: outline of an anarchistic theory of knowledge. London: Verso.

Frank, A.U. 1987. Overlay processing in spatial information systems. Proceedings AUTO-CARTO 8, 16-31.

Frank, A.U. 2001. Tiers of ontology and consistency constraints in GIS. *International Journal of Geographical Information Systems*, 15(7) 667-678.

Frank, A.U. 2012, GIS Theory – the fundamental principles in GIScience: A mathematical approach. In: Harvey (ed.) this volume.

Giere, R. 1999. *Science without Laws*. Chicago: University of Chicago Press.

Goodchild, M. F. 1992. Geographical information science. International *Journal of Geographical Information Systems*, 6(1), 31–45.

Goodchild, M.F. 2004. The validity and usefulness of laws in geographic information science and geography. *Annals of the AAG*, 94(2) 300-303.

Hacking, I. 1999. *The social construction of what?* Cambridge MA:

Harvard Press.

Harley, J. B. 1989. Deconstructing the map. *Cartographica*, 26(2), 1–20.

Harvey, F. and Chrisman, N. R. 1998. Boundary objects and the social construction of GIS technology. *Environment and Planning A*, 30, 1683–1694.

Harvey, F., and Chrisman, N.R. 2004. The Imbrications of Geography and Technology: The Social Construction of Geographic Information Systems. In: Brunn, Cutter & Harrington, eds. *Geography and Technology*. Dordrecht: Kluwer Academic Publishers, Chapter 4, pp. 65-80.

Hecht, B. and Moxley, E. 2009. Terabytes of Tobler: Evaluating the first law in a massive, domain-neutral representation of world knowledge. In: Hornsby, K.S., Claramunt, C., Denis, M., Ligozat, G., eds. Spatial Information Theory, COSIT 2009, Proceedings. Lecture Notes in Computer Science. Vol. 5756, Dordrecht: Springer pp. 88-105, .

Karnes, D. 1995. Modeling and Mapping New Metaphors: Towards Pluralistic Cartographies Using Object-Oriented Geographic Information Applications, PhD thesis, University of Washington, Seattle.

Kuhn, T.S. 1970. *The Structure of Scientific Revolutions*. second edition, Chicago: University of Chicago Press.

Lathrop, C. 1997. The Technical Aspects of International Maritime Boundary Delimitation, Depiction, and Recovery. Ocean Development and International Law, 28: 167-197.

Latour, B. 1993. *We Never Were Modern*. Cambridge MA: Harvard University Press.

Latour, B. 1999. *Pandora's Hope: Essays on the reality of science studies*. Cambridge MA: Harvard Press.

Latour, B. Jensen, P. Venturini T. Grauwin, S. and Bouiller, D., 2012. The whole is always smaller than its parts: A digital test of

Gabriel Tarde's Monads. British Journal of Sociology, in press.

Miller, H.J. 2004. Tobler's First Law and Spatial Analysis. *Annals of the AAG*, 94, 284-289.

Penrose, R., 1989. *The Emperors's New Mind: Concerning Computers, Minds and the Laws of Physics*. Oxford: Oxford University Press.

Poore, B.P. and Chrisman, N.R. 2006. Order from Noise: Towards a social theory of information, *Annals of the AAG* 96(3) 508–523.

Raper, J. 2000. *Multidimensional Geographic Information Science*. London: Taylor & Francis.

Robinson, A.H. and Petchenik, B.B. 1976. *The Nature of Maps: Essays toward understanding maps and mapping*. Chicago: University of Chicago Press.

Shapin, S, and Shaffer, S. 1985. *Leviathan and the Air Pump: Boyle, Hobbes, and the Experimental Life*. Princeton NJ, Princeton Press.

Sherman, J. and Tobler, W.R. 1957. The multiple use concept in cartography. *Professional Geographer*, 9(5): 5-7.

Sismondo, S. and Chrisman, N. R. 2001. Deflationary metaphysics and the natures of maps. *Philosophy of Science*, 68:S38–S49.

Sui, D. Z. 1999. GIS as media? Or how media theories can help us understand GIS and society. Geographic Information and Society (GISOC '99), Minneapolis, MN, 20–22 June.

Sui, D.Z. 2004. Tobler's First Law of Geography: A Big Idea for a Small World. *Annals of the AAG*, 94, 269-277

Sui, D.Z. and Goodchild, M.F. 2001. Are GIS becoming new media? *International Journal of Geographical Information Science*, 15(5), 387–90.

Tobler, W. R. 1959. Automation and cartography. *Geographical*

Review, 49, 526- 534.

Tobler, W.R. 1961. Map transformations of geographic space. PhD thesis, University of Washington, Seattle.

Tobler, W.R. 1969. Geographical filters and their inverses. *Geographical Analysis*, 1, 234- 253.

Tobler, WR. 1970. A computer movie simulating urban growth in the Detroit region. *Economic Geography*, 46, 234–40.

Tobler, W.R. 1976. Analytical cartography. *The American Cartographer*, 3, 21-31.

Tobler, W.R. 1979. A transformational view of cartography. *The American Cartographer*, 6, 101- 106.

Tobler, W.R. 2000. The development of analytical cartography: A personal note. *Cartography and Geographic Information Science*, 27 (3), 189–94.

Tobler, W.R. 2004. On the First Law of Geography: A Reply. *Annals of the AAG*, 94 304-310.

Zipf, G.K. 1949. *Human behavior and the principle of least effort.* Boston: Addison-Wesley.

Beyond mathematics and the deflationary turn: fundamental concepts in GIScience – to whom and for what ends?

Daniel Sui
The Ohio State University
Sui.10@osu.edu

The theme of the 2012 Tobler Lecture--fundamental concepts in GIScience--is closely in line with Tobler's life-long work. Indeed, this year not only coincides (approximately) with the 50th anniversary of the publication of Tobler's doctoral dissertation1 but also the 20th anniversary of Michael Goodchild's (1992) seminal paper, in which he first delineated the broad contours of then nascent GIScience. Thus, it is doubly fitting for the 2012 Tobler Lecture to reflect on fundamental concepts of GIScience.

I feel greatly honored to have served as a discussant for the 2012 Tobler Lecture. I knew at the outset, when I accepted the invitation, that it would be very challenging to comment on what Andrew Frank and Nick Chrisman have to say about the fundamental concepts in GIScience. I nonetheless had a lot of fun giving the presentation in New York City during the 2012 AAG meeting. I must confess, however, that I struggled quite a bit when I started writing this chapter because the deceptively simple question posed by Francis Harvey for this year's Tobler Lecture is, upon further reflection, immensely difficult, if not entirely impossible, to answer. Indeed, one could claim that almost the entire GIScience community has been trying to answer this question since the 1960s (e.g., Nystuen 1963), especially since Goodchild (1992) raised the banner of GIScience in 1992.

The goal of this chapter is two-fold: (1) to comment on the 2012 Tobler Lecture delivered by Andrew Frank and Nick Chrisman, and (2) to discuss both the convergent and divergent trends in GIScience and their implications for the development of fundamental concepts in GIScience, especially in the context of the recent big data deluge and emerging open science (Cribb and Hartomo 2010; Manyika et al. 2011; Nielsen 2012; Weinberg 2012). To achieve this dual goal, the rest of this paper is organized as follows. Section 1 comments on Frank's lecture, followed by a quick review of related work and problems and limitations of the formal/mathematical approach to GIScience. Section 2 comments on Chrisman's lecture, followed by a review of related literature on the deflationary turn and the consequences of the non-mathematical/critical approach to GIScience. Section 3 discusses centripetal and centrifugal forces in GIScience and their implications for the development of fundamental concepts in GIScience.

1. Andrew Frank's mathematical/formal approach and its discontents

Consistent with his lifelong work in GIScience, Frank's answer to the 2012 Tobler Lecture question is quite straightforward and unambiguous: yes, there are fundamental concepts in GIScience, which normally exist longer than the typical technological cycle, and--without apology--the holy grail for the development of these fundamental concepts/principles in GIScience is a mathematical and formal approach. I believe Frank did more than simply answer Harvey's deceptively simple question. Frank's chapter presents a grand vision of what an ideal GIS should be and what kinds of questions GIScience should answer.

According to Frank, GIS should move away from stasis, inherited from the past view of a GIS as a database of all potential maps or a repository of maps. Instead, GIS should be a spatial "time machine" with a focus on the representation of space/time processes. The fundamental principles in GIScience should be methods that allow us to combine various processes, from simple to complex ones. Although Frank does not deny the utility of other approaches to GIScience research, he argues that a mathematical/formal approach is the most viable for practicing GIScience. Frank provides support for his mathematical approaches using examples from map algebra, geometry, and tiered ontology.

Frank's emphasis on processes indicates he is keen to incorporate time and dynamics among the fundamental concepts in GIScience, while his stress on alternative geometries and topologies hints at his deep concern about different representations of space. Frank's tiered ontology covers both social and physical reality, aiming to synthesize and reason with imperfect information or indeterminate boundaries. Frank believes that space, time, complexity, tiered ontology, and synthesis (instead of analysis) should be treated as fundamentals in GIScience, and that we are more likely to tackle the field's fundamental challenges if we adopt a formal, mathematical, and mostly quantitative approach.

Frank clearly presents us with a very ambitious and comprehensive framework for thinking about the fundamental concepts and principles in GIScience. His chapter not only extends earlier work on the topic (Burrough and Frank 1995), but also provides a grand synthesis of his own work in GIScience during the past quarter century2. Undoubtedly, Frank's is a mainstream view of what fundamental principles and concepts in GIScience should be. His approach is supported by recent citation and social network analysis of the GIScience community (Skupin 2008; Sun and Manson 2011).

Using the ISI Web of Knowledge, Skupin (2008) identified the following researchers as the five most frequently cited in GIScience: Goodchild, Burrough, Egenhofer, Hutchinson, and Openshaw. In an updated study on the collaboration network using both Geobase and the ISI web of knowledge, Sun and Manson (2011) discovered that the following GIScientists have the most extensive collaborative social networks at the global level--Egenhofer, Goodchild, Lovett, Mark, Murray, and Shi. Those who follow the GIScience literature will immediately recognize that the top five most frequently cited GIScientists, as well as the six GIScientists who have the most extensive collaborative social networks, are all doing research consistent with Frank's vision of a mainstream GIScience research--formal, mathematical, and mostly quantitative or computational. Additionally, if we take a close look at the nineteen IJGIS classics Fisher (2006) put together, we will notice that, with the exception of three papers devoted to maps and visualization, the classics follow the mathematical/formal approach Frank describes in his chapter. I also find that the fundamental GIScience principles in Frank's chapter are remarkably consistent with Goodchid's (2010) inventory of major progress in GIScience during the past twenty years or so.

A mathematical/formal approach with quantitative and computational leanings has proven to be the mainstream approach for understanding GIScience and conducting research, and will perhaps continue to be so in the foreseeable future--as reflected in papers recently published in GIScience-related journals or presented during various GIScience meetings and conferences during the past five years. Nonetheless, I do not think that it is either realistic or desirable to frame GIScience exclusively from a mathematical/formal perspective. I believe this approach should be understood in terms of two broader contextual perspectives--the changing role of mathematics in scientific research, and the alternative motivations and drive for scientists to pursue scientific endeavors.

Throughout human history, mathematics has indisputably played a leading role in the development of multiple disciplines. Galileo Galilei (1967) even once remarked that the book of nature is perhaps written using the language of mathematics; indeed, to read the book of nature, one must grasp the language of mathematics (Calvino 1999). Or, consider physicist Eugene Wigner (1960), who invested mathematics with almost mystical power in his famous essay on the unreasonable effectiveness of mathematics in physical sciences. In short, mathematics has been given the "queen" status in the scientific world; for more than two centuries, the scientific world seems to have developed unshakable faith in the effectiveness of mathematics, and the mathematical approach has been regarded as the royal road to scientific truth--an outlook that received scant challenge until the mid-20th century. With Kurt Gödel's discovery of the incompleteness theorem (Dawson 2006), the late-20th century seems to have witnessed a sea change of attitude toward mathematics, which has been dethroned (Chaitin 1997). Instead of treating mathematics as a source of self-evident truth (almost transcendental), it was discovered that, at a very fundamental level, mathematics is based upon a set of metaphors (Lakoff and Nuñez 2001). In other words, math is also an embodied phenomenon--a creation of the human mind; just like all other human creations, mathematics, along with the formal approach attached to it, is socially constructed, with all of the attendant limitations and restrictions and subjectivities (Peat 1990), and thus must be understood as such instead of being treated as objective truth or unquestionably superior to other ways of knowing (Kneuper 1997).

Furthermore, it is now common knowledge among both scientists and science studies scholars that astonishing scientific discoveries are as often motivated by an attraction to the subject matter or an appreciation for beauty as by a motivation to seek truth (Chandrasekhar 1990; McAllister 1999; Miller 2002). In other words, roads leading to major scientific discoveries are often more artistic or imaginative, and not necessarily closely related to math or quantitative/formal methods, etc. In fact, as Bertrand Russell (1919) observed, even mathematics, rightly viewed, possesses "not only truth, but supreme beauty--a beauty cold and austere, like that of sculpture, without appeal to any part of our weaker nature, without the gorgeous trappings of painting or music, yet sublimely pure, and capable of a stern perfection such as only the greatest art can show" (60). Russell further argued that "the true spirit of delight, the exaltation, the sense of being more than Man, which is the touchstone of the highest excellence, is to be found in mathematics as surely as in poetry" (60).

As reflected in the recent literature, both these two trends (dethroning math/formal method as a superior way of knowing, and the revelation of alternative motivations for scientific discovery) have exerted their due influence on the development of GIScience, which led to a plethora of other alternative approaches for conducting GIScience (Cosgrove 2005; Sui 2005; Thrift 2005; Aitken and Craine 2006), especially the turn to seek aesthetic dimensions of data (Tufte 2006; Segaran and Hammmerbacher 2009). The faith in the unreasonable effectiveness of mathematics (Wigner 1960) is now being replaced with a belief in the unreasonable effectiveness of data (Halevy et al. 2009). These multiple alternative approaches for conducting GIScience constitute what Chrisman calls the deflationary turn in GIScience research.

2. Nick Chrisman's deflationary approach and its consequences

In contrast to Frank's grandiose vision for GIScience, Chrisman presents a more modest, anti-essentialist, anti-interpretive, deflationary stance on GIScience. According to Chrisman, the deflationary approach still "leaves room to compile a list of fundamental principles, but without grand claims of essentialism". By adopting a deflationary stance, Chrisman argues that we can tone down the rhetoric in the debates over fundamental principles, thus creating less tension between empirical work and the realm of theoretical debates. Some concepts/principles can/should serve as foundations (for the time being) for our educational/instructional endeavors, but claiming them as timeless universals is neither of great value nor importance.

Although Frank's mathematical/formal view on GIScience captured the hardcore (quantitative and computational) GIScience literature very well, the deflationary stance may be a more realistic depiction of what really happened in GIScience during the past twenty years on a broader scene. The deflationary stance is philosophically consistent with Feyerabend's (1975) approach for understanding science. In his best-known book, Against Method, Feyerabend argued, "Everywhere science is enriched by unscientific methods and unscientific results" (305–306), and that the very division between science and non-science was detrimental for true understanding. In retrospect, the deflationary turn in GIScience has made GIScience more inclusive and liberating as a form of social knowledge.

The development of GIS during the 1960s, and through the early-1990s, was heavily rooted in computer cartography, spatial databases, surveying and mapping, spatial analysis, and quantitative geography. Criticism from social theorists in the mid-1990s called forth a great broadening of the conceptual foundations of GIS (Sheppard 2005). Consequently, the past two decades witnessed a much more pluralistic development in the conceptual foundations of GIScience. Consistent with Couclelis's (1997) call to reconceptualize GIS without computers, GIScience researchers have drawn inspirations from a wide variety of disciplines and fields of inquiry, ranging from physics (Egenhofer and Mark 1995), complexity (Batty et al. 2012), biology (Shoval and Isaacson 2007), information theory (Poore and Chrisman 2006), operations research (http://www.spatial-or.com), computer science (Yang et al. 2012), to psychology (Fabrikant et al. 2002), philosophy/ontology (Couclelis 2010), economics (Sui 2008; Frank 2010), social theory (Pickles and Stallmann 2011), feminist studies (Pavlovskaya and Martin 2007), and hermeneutics (Gould 1994). GIScience scholars have borrowed concepts from the natural sciences, engineering/technical fields, the social/behavioral sciences, and the humanities. In place of exclusive reliance on the predominant quantitative/formal methods, GIScience researchers have developed a variety of new methods, ranging from qualitative GIS (Cope and Elwood 2009), and geonarrative approaches (Kwan and Ding 2008), to crowdsourcing (Shirky 2010; Sui et al. 2012), cyberGIS (Wang et al. 2012), and abduction approaches (Couclelis 2009).

If we probe more deeply into the meaning of the "G" in GIScience, GIScience has sought conceptual grounding in almost all the geographical paradigms developed so far (Agnew and Livingston 2011). Miller's (2007) people-based GIScience was conceptually inspired by Torsten Hägerstrand's time geography. Harvey (1997) traced the conceptual inspiration for overlay functions all the way back Hartshorne's geographic holism. Dobson (1993) found that Sauer's concept of landscape potentially serves as an integrating methodology, linking GIS, GPS, and remote sensing technologies. Anselin (2010) grounded his GeoDa toolbox entirely in the spatial dependence and spatial heterogeneity theme developed in regional science/spatial econometrics. Sui (1995) found Berry's geographic matrix, originally developed for regional synthesis, could serve as an illuminating pedagogical framework for teaching both with and about GIS. NCGIA's NSF-funded project to advance GIScience was aptly named after Bernhard Varenius--a seventeenth century geographer who wrote the first introductory textbook in general geography, Geographia Generalis, published first by Elsevier Press in 1650 (Warntz 1989). Most recently, due to the rapid growth of volunteered geographic information, there has been a subtle shift in emphasis from space to place in GIScience research. It is fascinating to note that all the marvelous technological advances have led people to practice geography as defined by Ptolmey (Sui 2009). Despite GIScience researchers' claim of innovation and new breakthroughs, and indeed there are plenty of those in a technical sense, GIScience is conceptually pretty paleo indeed (Curry 2001).

Generally speaking, the deflationary turn in GIScience has led to a more pluralistic development of GIScience. Without a clearly defined qualification (e.g., to whom and for what ends?), it is indeed very difficult to answer the question of what the fundamental concepts and principles in GIScience are. I concur with Clarke's (2012) assessment that currently there still exists no general theory about geographic information, despite efforts in this area (Goodchild et al. 2007). Perhaps the only thing we are certain of regarding spatial data is its uncertainty (Couclelis 2004). By probing the ontological and epistemological assumptions of various scientific practices, Habermas (1972) grouped all scientific endeavors into three major kinds--the empirical/analytic, the hermeneutic, and the critical sciences. GIScience has evolved along all of these three dimensions during the past twenty years. Frank's approach to GIScience represents predominantly the empirical/analytic strand of GIScience. But, by taking a more deflationary stance, we can better understand and more deeply appreciate GIScience from empirical, hermeneutic, and critical perspectives.

3. Centripetal and Centrifugal forces in GIScience: fundamental concepts in GIScience in the age of big data and open science

The development of a discipline often follows a paradoxical process of simultaneous convergence and fragmentation, due to the existence of both centripetal and centrifugal forces. To be a viable discipline in the academy, a set of core fundamental concepts must be developed and widely accepted, but, ironically, this centripetal process for developing a set of core concepts for a discipline itself often turns into a centrifugal one. Perhaps analogous to the dual characteristics of spatial processes--dependence and heterogeneity (Anselin 1989)-- the intellectual landscape of GIScience has simultaneously undergone both convergence and divergence as both centripetal and centrifugal forces shape its development. It is this dual process of crystallization and fragmentation that ultimately propels the development of GIScience, as has happened in many other disciplines.

By necessity (for both sociological and intellectual reasons), a discipline must contain certain core concepts in order to justify or legitimize its existence in the academy. These core concepts are usually covered in the textbooks related to the discipline, or reflected in the curriculum materials. Despite its relative short history, I believe GIScience has succeeded admirably in developing both textbooks and curriculum materials that establish and maintain its "core". We now have more than a dozen well-written GIScience textbooks available on the market in multiple languages, all systematically presenting the fundamental concepts of GIScience. Collectively, the GIScience community has devoted considerable time and energy to the development of GIScience curriculum materials, as first exemplified in the GIScience core curriculum led by NCGIA (http://www.ncgia.ucsb.edu/education/projects/core.php), and then followed by the GIScience body of knowledge led by UCGIS (DiBiase et al. 2002). Recently, following the crowdsourcing mode, we have also witnessed the emergence of websites devoted exclusively to teaching fundamental spatial concepts, such as teachspatial.org, visual-learners.com, and spatialroundtable.com. Through these centripetal forces, GIScience has--during the past twenty years--converged towards a set of core concepts. However, upon close scrutiny, these core concepts also reveal considerable diversity and divergence. For example, the GIScience body of knowledge project led by UCGIS has identified a diverse range of fundamental concepts, which have been put into five general categories: conceptual foundation, data modeling, analytical methods, design aspects, and visualization (DiBiase et al. 2002). Under each category, there are multiple layers of concepts and topics. Without qualifying this year's Tobler Lecture question "fundamental" to whom and for what purposes, it is almost impossible to pick any of the more-than 170 concepts as "fundamental" concepts for GIScience. Furthermore, the research enterprise itself is centrifugal because, if we want to be innovative researchers, we must, by necessity, think outside the box, challenge the orthodoxy, or, in other words, move away from the established conceptual core.

Compared to the long histories of cartography and geography, the short history of GIScience (approximately twenty to fifty years) is almost negligible, but it nonetheless has shown remarkable similarities with that of cartography. As Edney (1993) argued so cogently for the history of cartography in his well-known "cartography without progress" thesis, we will be terribly ill-informed if we view the history of cartography as monolithic and linear, progressing from inaccurate/incomplete maps to more accurate/complete ones. Instead, it is more realistic and productive to view the development of cartography as "a complex amalgam of different modes, situated in different cultural, social, and technological relationships" (Edney, 1993, p.54). According to Edney (1993), these different modes are best understood as responses to particular, and often local, contexts, careful consideration of which would illustrate the rich potential of an anti-progressive approach to the development of cartography. I see a similar dynamics in the case of GIScience, albeit at a much shorter temporal (and perhaps smaller geographical) scale.

In summary, let's get back to where we started with this year's Tobler Lecture question: are there fundamental concepts in GIScience? Both Frank and Chrisman have answered this deceptively simple question eloquently. Although their answers seem to be different on the surface, I believe they are closely connected (and converging) in a deeper sense. As pioneering and practicing GIScientists, both Frank and Chrisman have recognized the importance of developing fundamental concepts in GIScience beyond the technological boom and bust. If I can borrow Longino's (2002) vocabulary, Frank's approach is more in line with the rational model, whereas Chrisman's leans toward a social approach for GIScience knowledge production. As Longino (2002) has demonstrated with respect to several other disciplines, the dichotomy between the rational and the social approach for knowledge production is often misguided and can be bridged through meaningful interaction/engagement. In fact, to address all the conceptual issues Frank envisions for GIS and GIScience, relying exclusively on a mathematical approach will not be sufficient; we must be more inclusive of alternative approaches-- in other words, we must be deflationary in our philosophical/

methodological outlook. Frank has actually practiced this approach himself as he developed qualitative approaches for GIScience or borrowed perspectives from other disciplines (e.g., economics). As for Chrisman's more deflationary, social approach to GIScience, practitioners should realize that a mathematical/formal approach may also be needed; qualitative work only goes so far. As was the case for Frank, Chrisman's trajectory also confounds the social and cognitive/rational distinction, particularly in his reliance on the formal/mathematical approach during the early days of GIS.

According to Goodchild (2011), if there is a single challenging issue in GIScience research, it is this: "to find useful and efficient ways of capturing and representing the infinite complexity of the geographical domain in the limited space and binary alphabet of a digital computer" (12). GIScience researchers have discovered multiple ways to address this challenging issue through a variety of rational/cognitive and deflationary/social approaches, and will most likely continue to do so in the future. Like Galison (1998) and Harvey (2005), I believe productive trading zones exist between different approaches for knowledge production in GIScience. The current big data deluge will further demand active trading between GIScientists of different philosophical and methodological approaches. The emerging open science paradigm will greatly facilitate the trading, possibly moving us on a faster track to better understand the world (and ourselves) through GIScience.

In late March 2012, the Obama White House announced multiple new federal initiatives that specifically target the challenges created by the big data deluge (http://www.whitehouse.gov/sites/default/files/

microsites/ostp/big_data_press_release.pdf). The push for a new paradigm under the general umbrella "open science" deserves our attention. Efforts devoted to open science are quickly fleshing out the details of emerging data-intensive inquiries (otherwise known as the Fourth paradigm (Hey et al. 2009). Despite diverse interpretations of the precise meaning of open science (e.g., open source, open data, open access, open notebook, or networked science), the emerging open science paradigm, in a nutshell, includes the following basic principles (Gezelter 2009), which will be influential for the development of GIScience in the next twenty years:

* Transparency in methods of data collection, observation, and experiments;

* Public availability and reusability of scientific data to facilitate reproducibility;

* Public accessibility of scientific communication and publication;

* Mass collaboration involving both experts and amateurs/citizens using web-based tools.

To move forward, I believe that the emerging open science paradigm in GIScience (Jiang 2011) will be driven by similar centripetal and centrifugal forces. On the one hand, an open GIScience will call and push for more trading between GIScience and multiple other fields in science, engineering, and the humanities. On the other hand, these centrifugal development efforts will lead to a new round of efforts for standards and interoperability. I believe that a new set of fundamental concepts and principles in GIScience will emerge through the tensions created by the centrifugal and centripetal forces in GIScience development. GIScience must change with time, otherwise it will age (and eventually die) in place (Wilson and Ramasubramanian 2011).

Endnotes

1. Tober's Ph.D. dissertation was published in 1961, entitled "Map Transformations of Geographic Space," University of Washington, Seattle, 1961, 183 pp; University Microfilms No. 61 – 4011.

2. For a full list Andrew Frank's publications, please visit his website at: http://www.geoinfo.tuwien.ac.at/staff/index.php? Current_Staff:Frank%2C_Andrew_U (accessed May 1, 2012).

Acknowledgement

Thanks are due to Nick Crane, Xining Yang, and Wenqin Chen for research assistance. Comments by Francis Harvey on an earlier draft also significantly improved this chapter. The author is solely responsible for any remaining errors.

References

Agnew, J.A. and Livingstone, D.N., eds., 2011. Sage Handbook of Geographical Knowledge. London: Sage Publications.

Aitken, S. and Craine, J., 2006. Affective geovisualizations [online]. Directions Magazine.

Anselin, L., 1989. What is special about spatial data? Alternative perspectives on spatial data analysis [online]. Available from: http://www.drs.wisc.edu/documents/articles/

curtis/cesoc977/anselin1989.pdf [Accessed 21 February 2012].

Anselin, L., 2010. From SpaceStat to CyberGIS, twenty years of spatial data analysis software. International Regional Science

Review, 35, 131-57.

Barnes, T.J. and Sheppard, E., 2010. 'Nothing includes everything': Towards engaged pluralism in Anglophone economic geography. Progress in Human Geography, 34(2), 193–214.

Batty, M., R. Morphet, P. Masucci, and K. Stanilov, 2012. Entropy, complexity and spatial information. CASA Working Paper Series, available on-line at: http://www.bartlett. ucl.ac.uk/casa/pdf/paper185 [Accessed on May 20, 2012].

Burrough, P.A. and Frank, A.U.,1995. Concepts and paradigms in spatial information: Are current geographic information systems truly generic? International Journal of Geographic Information Science,9(2), 101-116.

Calvino, I., 1999. The book of nature in Galileo. In I. Calvino, Why Read the Classics? (pp. 83-89). New York: Pantheon Books.

Chaitin, G.J., 1997. The limits of mathematics: A course on information theory and the limits of formal reasoning. Berlin, Springer.

Chandrasekhar, S., 1990. Truth and beauty: Aesthetics and motivations in science. Chicago, IL.: University of Chicago Press.

Clarke, K.C., 2012. Is there a theory of geographic information? GeoJournal(forthcoming).

Cope, M and Elwood, S., 2009. Qualitative GIS: A mixed methods approach. London: SAGE Publications.

Cosgrove, D., 2005. Maps, mapping, modernity: Art and cartography in the twentieth century. Imago Mundi, 57 (1): 35-54.

Couclelis, H., 1997. GIS without computers: Building geographic information science from the ground up. In: Z. Kemp,K., ed. Innovations in GIS - 4: Selected papers from the Fourth National Conference on GIS Research UK (GISRUK). London: Taylor &

Francis, 219-26.

Couclelis, H., 2004. The certainty of uncertainty. ransactions in GIS, 7 (2), 165-175.

Couclelis, H., 2009. The abduction of geographic information science: Transporting spatial reasoning to the realm of purpose and design. In: K.S. Hornsby, C. Claramunt, M. Denis, and G. Ligozat, eds. Spatial information theory, 9th international conference, COSIT 2009. Berlin: Springer, 342-356.

Couclelis, H., 2010. Ontologies of geographic information. International Journal of Geographical Information Science, 24 (12), 1785-1809.

Cribb, J. and T. S. Hartomo, 2010. Open science: Sharing knowledge in the global century. Collingwood, Australia: CSRIO Publishing.

Dawson, J.W., 2006. Gödel and the limits of logic [online]. Plus+ Magazine. Available from: http://plus.maths.org/content/goumldel-and-limits-logic.

DiBiase, D., DeMers, M., Johnson, A., Kemp, K., Luck, A. T., Plewe, B., and Wentz, E., eds., 2002. Geographic information science and technology body of knowledge. Washington DC: Association of American Geographers.

Dobson, J.E., 1993. A conceptual framework for integrating remote sensing, GIS, and geography. Photogrammetric Engineering and Remote Sensing 59 (10), 1491–96.

Edney, M.H., 1993. Cartography without 'progress': Reinterpreting the nature of and historical development of mapmaking. Cartographica, 30 (2/3): 54-68. Fisher, P.F., 2006. Classics from IJGIS: Twenty years of the International Journal of Geographical Information Science and Systems. Boca Raton, FL.: CRC Press.

Egenhofer, M. and D. Mark, 1995. Naïve geography. In A. Frank and

W. Kuhn (eds.), COSIT `95, Lecture Notes in Computer Science, vol. 988. Berlin: Springer-Verlag, 1-15.

Fabrikant, S., D.R. Montello, M. Ruocco, and R. Middleton, 2002. The first Law of cognitive geography: Distance and similarity in semantic space. Paper presented during GIScience 2002, Sept. 25-28, Boulder, Colorado.

Frank, A.U., 2010. Eight Nobel laureates' contribution to GIScience. Keynote Lecture for GeoValue 2010, Hamburg, Germany, Jan. 10, 2010.

Galilei, G. 1967. Dialogue Concerning the Two Chief World Systems -- Ptolemaic and Copernican. Berkeley: University of California Press.

Galison, P. ,1998. Image and logic. Cambridge, MA: Harvard University Press.

Gezelter, D., 2009. What, exactly, is Open Science? [online]. Available from: http://www.openscience.org/blog/?p=269.

Goodchild, M.F., 1992. Geographical information science. International Journal of Geographical Information Systems, 6 (1), 31–45.

Goodchild, M.F., 2010. Twenty years of progress: GIScience in 2010. Journal of Spatial Information Science, 1 (1), 3–20.

Goodchild, M.F., 2011. Challenges in geographical information science. Proceedings of the Royal Society A. rspa.2011.0114v1-rspa20110114

Goodchild, M.F., Yuan, M., and Cova, T.J., 2007. Towards a general theory of geographic representation in GIS. International Journal of Geographical Information Science, 21 (3), 239–260.

Gould, M.D., 1994. GIS design: A hermeneutic view. Photogrammetric Engineering and Remote Sensing, 60 (9),

1105-1116.

Habermas, J., 1972. Knowledge and human interests. London: Heinemann.

Halevy, A., Norvig, P., and Pereira, P., 2009. The unreasonable effectiveness of data. IEEE Intelligent Systems, March/April, 8-12.

Harvey, F. 1997. From geographic holism to geographic information system. The Professional Geographer, 49 (1), 77–85.

Harvey, F., 2005. The linguistic trading zones of semantic interoperability. In P. F. Fisher and D. J. Unwin (eds.), Re-presenting GIS. Chichester, England: John Wiley and Sons, 43-55.

Hey, T., Tansley, S., and Tolle, K., eds., 2009. The Fourth Paradigm: Data-intensive Scientific Discovery. Redmond, WA: Microsoft Research.

Jiang, B., 2011. Making GIScience research more open access. International Journal of Geographical Information Science, 25 (8), 1217–1220.

Kneuper, R., 1997. Limits of formal methods [online]. Available from: http://www.kneuper.eu/English/Publications/limits-formal-methods.pdf.

Kwan, M.-P. and G. Ding. 2008. Geo-narrative: Extending geographic information systems for narrative analysis in qualitative and mixed-method research. The Professional Geographer, 60(4), 443-465.

Longino, H., 2002. The fate of knowledge. Princeton, N.J.: Princeton University Press.

Manyika, J., Chui, M., Brown, B., Bughin, J., Dobbs, R., Roxburgh, C., and Byers, A.H., 2011. Big data: The next frontier for innovation, competition, and productivity [online]. Available from: http://

www.mckinsey.com/Insights/

MGI/Research/Technology_and_Innovation/ Big_data_The_next_frontier_for_innovation.

McAllister, J.A., 1999. Beauty and revolution in science. Ithaca, N.Y.: Cornell University Press.

Miller, A., 2002. Einstein, Picasso: Space, time and the beauty that causes havoc. New York: Basic Books.

Miller, H., 2007. Place-based versus people-based geographic information science. Geography Compass, 1(3), 503–535.

Nielsen, M., 2012. Reinventing discovery: The new era of networked science. Princeton, N.J.: Princeton University Press.

Nystuen, J.D., 1963. Identification of some fundamental spatial concepts. Michigan Academy of Science, Arts, and Letters, 48, 373–384.

Pavlovskaya, M. and K.S. Martin, 2007. Feminism and geographic information systems: From a missing object to a mapping subject. Geography Compass, 1(3), 583–606.

Peat, F.D., 1990. Mathematics and the language of nature. [online]. In: R.E. Mickens, ed. Mathematics and sciences. (Word scientific, 1990). Available from: http://www.fdavidpeat.com/bibliography/ essays/maths.htm#bib9.

Pickles, J. and Stallmann, T., 2011. Mapping and social theory. In: M. Monmonier, ed. The history of cartography: Twentieth century. Chicago: Chicago University Press.

Poore, B.S. and N. R. Chrisman, 2006. Order from noise: Toward a social theory of geographic information. Annals of the Association of American Geographers, 96 (3), 508–523.

Russell, B., 1919. The study of mathematics. Orgingially published in Mysticism and logic: And other essays. London, Longman: 58-73 (available on-line: books.google.com)

Segaran, T. and Hammerbacher, J., 2009. Beautiful data: The stories behind elegant data solutions. Sebastopol., CA: O'Reilly.

Sheppard, E., 2005. Knowledge production through critical GIS: Review and assessment. Cartographica, 40, 5-22.

Shirky, C., 2010. Cognitive surplus: How technology makes consumers into collaborators. New York: Penguin.

Shoval, N. and M. Isaacson, 2007. Sequence alignment as a method for human activity analysis in space and time. Annals of the Association of American Geographers, 97(2), 282-297.

Skupin, A., 2008. NCGIA@20. Presentations made during the International Symposium on Geographic Information Science, Dec. 10-13, available on-line at: http://ncgia.ucsb.edu/projects/isgis/docs/ Skupin-reunion-presentation.pdf (last accessed on May 1, 2012).

Steiniger, S. and Hunter, A., 2012. Geospatial free and open source software in the 21st century. Lecture notes in geoinformation and cartography, Part 5. Berlin: Springer, 247-261.

Sui, D. Z., 1995. A new pedagogic framework to link GIS to geography's intellectual core. Journal of Geography 94(6), 578-591.

Sui, D., 2005. Beethoven, Picasso and GIS: Is spatial really special? GeoWorld, September, 22-24.

Sui, D., 2008. Geography and the Nobel prize. GeoWorld, December Issue, 17-19.

Sui, D., 2009. Rethinking Ptolemy in the age of Web 2.0: Neogeography is paleo. GeoWorld, March Issue, 23-25.

Sui, D., Elwood, S., and Goodchild, M.F., eds., 2012. Crowdsourcing geographic knowledge: Volunteered geographic information in theory and practice. Berlin: Springer.

Sun, S. and Manson, S., 2011. Social network analysis of the academic GIscience community. The Professional Geographer, 63 (1): 18-33.

TeachSpatial.org, 2011. Concepts of spatial thinking - by category 2011 [online]. Available from: http://www.teachspatial.org/ fundamental-concepts-spatial-thinking.

Thrift, N., 2005. Torsten Hägerstrand and social theory. Progress in Human Geography, 337-340.

Tufte, E.R. 2006. Beautiful evidence. Cheshire, CT.: Graphics Press.

Warntz, W., 1989. Newton, the Newtonians, and the Geographia Generalis Varenii. Annals of the Association of American Geographers 79(2), 165-191.

Weinberger, D., 2012. Too big to know: Rethinking knowledge now that the facts aren't the facts, experts are everywhere, and the smartest person in the room is the room. New York: Basic Books.

Wigner, E.P., 1960. The unreasonable effectiveness of mathematics in the natural sciences. Communications on Pure and Applied Mathematics, 13, 1–14.

Wilson, J.P. and Ramasubramanian, L., 2011. GIS: A field that is changing with the times or one that is aging in place? [online]. Directions Magazine. Available from: http:// www.directionsmag.com/articles/gis-a-field-that-is-changing-with-the-times-or-one-that-is-aging-in-pl/199277 [Accessed 21 April 2012].

Yang C., Goodchild M., Huang Q., Nebert D., Raskin R., Bambacus M., Xu Y., Fay D., 2011. Spatial cloud computing – How can geospatial sciences use and help to shape cloud computing. International Journal of Digital Earth, 4(4), 305-329.

Afterword

Michael F. Goodchild
University of California, Santa Barbara
good@geog.ucsb.edu

It's an honor to be asked to write an afterword to this collection, especially since I wasn't able to attend the Tobler Lecture in New York in February 2012 because of a conflict with a parallel session. I like the question, and I am fascinated by the ways Andrew Frank and Nick Chrisman chose to address it, as well as by the perspective added by Dan Sui. An afterword is in principle the last word in the book, but it also implies an obligation to look forward, so perhaps I could offer some comments in both contexts.

One might expect the question "Are there principles in geographic information science?" to be addressed by attempting to enumerate those principles, and by a simple answer of "yes" or "no", depending on whether the list of enumerated principles was at least of length two (or perhaps length one, if we ignore the fine distinction of the plural). The fact that none of the authors chose this approach says much about their ability to weave interesting stories around simple questions, which is of course a mark of the true academic, but more on that anon. Dan Sui chose to elaborate the question by adding "(and) to whom and for what ends?", by which I assume he means "fundamental to whom?" and "for what ends should we enumerate these principles?" (I am ignoring any implied distinction between the principles of the original question and the concepts of Dan Sui's title).

To my mind, the acid test of whether principles exist in a discipline comes in education, in deciding how to organize a curriculum and how to teach a course. Principles provide the basic foundation to any course and the basis of its "learning outcomes", to use a current but

Are there fundamental principles in GIScience?

somewhat mechanistic term. I cannot imagine how I would teach a course that was not founded on principles, or how I would examine what a student learned from such a course. In GIS, we have long recognized the difference between training, emphasizing the manipulation of the user interface of this year's version of the technology, and education, which emphasizes the principles that will be as true in twenty years as they are today. So, it seems to me that the easiest way to answer the question is to identify the principles that ground the courses I teach in GIScience. From that perspective, the answer to the question is a resounding "yes".

Tobler's First Law of Geography (TFL) has rightly been cited in the preceding chapters, and, by any measure, it constitutes a fundamental principle of GIScience. It is deceptive in the informality of its wording, but it is of course no more and no less than a colloquial statement of the mathematical principle that underlies all of geostatistics and spatial statistics. In those fields, it is formalized and operationalized in various metrics of spatial dependence, and I firmly support Andrew Frank in his argument that principles are best expressed mathematically. However, I think the plain-language version also has its own value and charm, especially in teaching GIScience, because we cannot assume that our students will be either skilled in mathematics or sympathetic to it.

I like to imagine a world without TFL, in which a movement of a fraction of a centimeter might in principle encounter the entire range of conditions observed on the Earth's surface, from the depths of the Marianas Trench to the top of Everest, and from the temperatures in winter at the South Pole to those in New Delhi in June. From such a perspective, I like to say that TFL has at least as much relevance to life on Earth as the Second Law of Thermodynamics. Against that perspective, Nick Chrisman's use of TFL to advocate a paradigm of deflation seems odd to me, in that it makes two assumptions: first, that TFL is a fundamental principle and thus the answer to the session's central question is "yes", and second that it has been over-inflated (to deflate a balloon, it is first necessary to inflate it). To me, quite the opposite is true: TFL languished in obscurity for decades after its original assertion, and it is only recently that we have begun to understand its true import.

TFL is an empirical principle, derived from and found to be generally consistent with observation, and thus firmly in the tradition of all empirical sciences. Why it should be so generally true raises profound questions about the relative strength of smoothing and sharpening processes on the Earth's surface. It has important corollaries, some of which deserve recognition in their own right. Consider, for example, the nature of positional error. Like any measurement, it is impossible to measure position on the Earth's surface exactly (perhaps itself a fundamental principle), and all positions are subject to error. But, because nearby errors tend to be positively correlated, short distances calculated from coordinates tend to be more accurate than long distances. One might express this in the statement "Relative positional error is almost always less than absolute error", implying that the shapes of features tend to be preserved much better than they would be if their vertices were subject to independent positional errors.

Cartographic generalization also leads to some fundamental principles. Mandelbrot's fractal principle (Mandelbrot 1982) asserts that many types of geographic features reveal more detail the more closely one looks, and do so at a predictable rate if the feature's geometry is self-similar. The computed length of a polyline in GIS also shrinks as the feature is generalized for similar reasons, and so must almost always be treated as an underestimate. Spatial cognition is also a rich field to mine for fundamental principles of GIScience.

Other principles are less empirical and perhaps thus more compatible with Andrew Frank's central argument in support of mathematics, being derived by logical argument. This mix of empiricism and logic is to me one of the many attractions of GIScience as a field, one of the characteristics that distinguish it from other disciplines, and consequently what makes it important in the education of GIScientists. Among principles derived by logical and mathematical argument, I would list the concepts of continuous fields and discrete objects, along with the modifiable areal unit problem and its close relative the ecological fallacy. Egenhofer's 9-intersection (Egenhofer and Franzosa 1991) must also rank highly as a fundamental principle of GIScience, and of spatial information science more broadly. Hierarchical structures such as the quadtree (Samet 1990) and the family of discrete global grids (Sahr, White, and Kimerling 2003) also seem sufficiently non-intuitive to merit inclusion in a list of the fundamental principles of GIScience.

Anselin's much-cited response to the question "What's special about spatial?" (Anselin 1989) has two components: TFL, and a principle of spatial heterogeneity. Although the former has received much greater attention, the latter seems to me even more important in some respects, especially in its implications for public policy. It is the principle behind the push towards local or place-based spatial analysis, as represented by geographically weighted regression (Fotheringham, Brunsdon, and Charlton 2002). It is the reason why local standards will always conflict with global ones, and why projects to harmonize local standards, such as the European Union's INSPIRE, are so problematic. It also explains why the nomothetic goal, of general principles that apply everywhere in space and time, is so difficult to achieve in the social and environmental sciences.

Given this richness, it is puzzling to me that it was felt necessary to ask the session's core question, and that the main protagonists chose not to address it by simply listing principles. I have encountered several instances recently of this kind of reluctance, and would cite the ambivalence of many of the contributions to the 2004 Annals forum on TFL (Sui 2004), and the very mixed responses to a similar question asked at the twentieth anniversary meeting of NCGIA in 2008 (http://ncgia.ucsb.edu/projects/isgis/; Goodchild 2010). It seems to me that the field is badly in need of a bout of inflation rather than deflation if it is ever to hold its head high as a discipline.

Dan Sui's supplementary "for whom" seems especially appropriate at this point: GIScientists need to be able to explain to others why their field constitutes a science, to detail what it has discovered about its subject matter, and to explain why pursuing its research agenda will benefit science and society at large. Every year, each new Fellow of the Royal Society is given fifteen minutes to talk about what he or she does to an audience that regularly includes Nobel laureates. In my case, my fifteen minutes, in London in 2010, followed a mathematician from Cambridge who had made new discoveries in the theory of prime numbers. The written version of my presentation was later published in the Proceedings of the Royal Society (Goodchild 2011). I humbly suggest that deflation would have been a disastrous paradigm to adopt in this context.

So what of the future? I wish I could point interested colleagues in other disciplines to a concise summary of the fundamental principles of GIScience. I understand that at least one monograph on that topic is in preparation, but today's GIS texts, excellent as many are, still mix the technical details of today's technology with fundamental principles, often making the latter hard to find. In my case, an understanding of fundamental principles emerged only slowly after years of working with the technology. As the technology has become easier to use, and as many GIS functions are now available through simple user interfaces, we have the opportunity to place more emphasis on fundamental principles and concepts--to put the horse finally in front of the cart. I doubt we will ever agree on a single list, but let us at least agree that it is important that we as individuals make our own lists. I think we can be confident that some degree of commonality will emerge from the exercise.

References

Anselin, L. 1989. What is special about spatial data? Alternative perspectives on spatial data analysis. Technical Report 89-4. Santa Barbara, CA: National Center for Geographic Information and Analysis.

Egenhofer, M. J. and R. D. Franzosa 1991. Point-set topological relations. *International Journal of Geographical Information Systems* 5(2): 161-174.

Fotheringham, A. S., C. Brunsdon, and M. Charlton 2002. *Geographically Weighted Regression: The Analysis of Spatially Varying Relationships*. Hoboken, NJ: Wiley.

Goodchild, M. F. 2010. Twenty years of progress: GIScience in 2010. *Journal of Spatial Information Science* 1: 3-20.

Goodchild, M. F. 2011. Challenges in geographical information science. *Proceedings of the Royal Society A* 467(2133): 2431-2443.

Mandelbrot, B. 1982. *The Fractal Geometry of Nature*. San Francisco: Freeman.

Sahr, K., D. White, and A. J. Kimerling 2003. Geodesic discrete global grid systems. *Cartography and Geographic Information Science* 30(2): 121-134.

Samet, H. 1990. *The Design and Analysis of Spatial Data Structures*. Reading, MA: Addison-Wesley.

Sui, D. Z. 2004. Tobler's first law of geography: A big idea for a small world. *Annals of the Association of American Geographers* 94: 269-277.